The 2 oz. Backpacker

Other Ten Speed Press Books
by Robert S. Wood

DESOLATION WILDERNESS
MOUNTAIN CABIN
PLEASURE PACKING FOR THE '80's

ABOUT THE AUTHOR

Long a tinkerer with backpacking equipment and a searcher
after comfort in the wilds, Robert S. Wood has been walking
and climbing for twenty-five years in the Sierra Nevada, the
Cascades, Mexico, Europe, South America, New Zealand and
Australia. He has written and edited for a number of maga-
zines, including *Time, Life, Sports Illustrated, Sierra Club
Bulletin, Wilderness Camping* and *Outside*.

The 2 oz. Backpacker

by Robert S. Wood

Drawings by Warren Dayton
and the author

Cover by the author

Ten Speed Press

For my Mother
Helen S. Wood

1🖐

TEN SPEED PRESS
P. O. Box 7123
Berkeley, California 94707

Library of Congress Catalog Number: 82-80236
ISBN: 0-89815-070-1

Book Design by Hal Hershey
Cover Illustration by Jon Larson

Printed in the United States of America

7 8 9 10 — 93 92 91

CONTENTS

Introduction
7

ONE
Walking
9

TWO
Keeping Fit
45

INTRODUCTION
The 2 oz. Backpacker?

Readers have asked for a featherweight source book they can justify carrying along with them in the wilds, something that will provide a backup to their own experience, help them deal with adversity and ensure their getting the most from their trips.

That's exactly what I've tried to produce. This little book deals exclusively with situations backpackers encounter in wilderness. Here are the tips and techniques my friends and I use to sail along safe and easy in the wilds, staying out of trouble, getting the maximum pleasure and comfort from our trips.

I've tried to cram all the data I can into a small, tough, flexible format on light, thin but high quality paper, aiming at a total book weight of just two ounces, so weight-conscious backpackers will carry it. If the printer failed "to make the weight" you can always rip off the covers or take scissors to the margins.

This is strictly a field guide. I have wasted no space on data that can't help you in the wilds. If you want to know how to choose the right gear, get in shape, travel light, select clothing, plan menus and trips, and understand how insulators, fabrics and the human body interact, get my *Pleasure Packing for the 80's*, also from Ten Speed. It's a soup to nuts, 255 page reference book on backpacking, but it weighs twelve ounces and isn't meant to be carried. Much of this little book has been distilled from its best selling big brother.

This isn't a survival booklet, either. A backpacker shouldn't need to know how to rub two sticks together for fire, flag down a passing plane, snare rabbits or cook without pots. He's supposed to have all the essentials on his back and be prepared to travel through the country he has chosen to visit. This little book is to help you deal with discomfort, injury or other emergency. It's also to help you maximize your safety and minimize your worry, to provide an extra margin of safety. Think of it as you do emergency food, bandages, surplus matches and extra batteries. You hope you won't need them, but you don't dare leave them home!

I've tried to organize my material for easy access, so you can find what you need without reading the whole book. The chapter headings have been supplemented (both in the table of contents and at the head of each chapter) with an elaboration of what's contained. Headlines within the text match this elaboration to help you with equipment breakdown, unexpected weather, unfriendly campsites or a temporary loss of orientation. You can likewise find techniques to help you wring the most pleasure from your precious vacation.

Even if you don't get in trouble twenty miles from nowhere, this little book will have its uses. The blank pages in back, used for notes, can double the pleasure of your next trip by reminding you what to leave home, what to bring more of and what to do differently. Or leave notes to your partner or a record in mountaintop registers. The text can supply escape reading on a rainy afternoon in the tent. It will even function as inferior toilet or cigarette paper, or excellent firestarter after a rain. Or you can prop up the stove with it, patch a hole in your boot or insulate your bottom while sitting on cold rocks. And if you're desperate enough it can even be boiled in salted water to make a low calorie broth.

Whatever uses you find for this little book, I hope it helps you to a happier, safer trip when you're deep in the wilds with only the pack you carry on your back.

Bob Wood
Walker, California
March 1982

ONE
Walking

This little book is meant to be carried with you in the wilds, to help you out when you need help, cheer you up when you're tired and make you more comfortable. I sincerely hope you find what you need.

A backpacker's ability to walk efficiently, safely and comfortably is absolutely vital to a happy trip. And walking well is no joke when you must make your way through wild country, often on steep and difficult terrain, under widely varying weather conditions, sometimes at high altitude, carrying everything you need on your back. Fortunately, there are ways to make wilderness travel a lot easier, safer and more fun.

There is a myth that one should find a comfortable pace and then stick to it. Nothing could be farther from the truth. The most common error among hikers is trying doggedly to maintain a set pace despite changes in the grade. Constant speed is an impossible goal. Comfortable, efficient walking depends on maintaining one's energy output—not one's speed—at a level which will not produce excessive fatigue. This simply means slowing down when the trail climbs, then speeding up when it levels off.

The length of one's stride should also be variable. When the trail suddenly grows steeper, I not only slow down, I take shorter steps. When the trail levels off, my stride gradually lengthens. Walking in this manner, i.e. trying to maintain an even and comfortable output of energy rather than trying to maintain a constant speed, I am never forced to stop from exhaustion, and I log more miles per day in greater comfort.

There's a scientific basis for my "variable speed" philosophy. Specialists have determined that for every individual and set of walking conditions there is an *ideal* pace, an optimal speed which requires minimal energy per step. Our internal computer instinctively tries to conserve energy and it will govern our speed for maximum efficiency—if we let it! Ignoring the clockwork within ourselves—by hurrying and even by moving too slowly—will be far more tiring than the optimal pace because it's using more energy than necessary.

Finding an Ideal Pace

Since every individual will have a different ideal speed, group travel presents certain problems. A 5'2" lady complained, "My 6'3" boyfriend, who is normally very thoughtful, spent a lot of time on our backpacking trip bawling me out for being slow, clumsy and lazy—none of which I am if I'm accepted at my size and weight. It took me three steps for every two of his." Her boyfriend complained about his 40 pound pack, though it was only 20% of his weight, while she struggled to keep up carrying 25 pounds, fully 25% of her hundred pound weight. This couple was trapped into a mutually unhappy situation by his failure to understand their different physical capacities and by the less obvious but more common assumption that they had to travel together—which means at the same speed.

How Much to Carry?

Because of their construction and chemical makeup, women are at a disadvantage carrying a pack in the wilds— quite apart from their lesser size and weight. Couples determined to hike together can best equalize the situation by adjusting their loads. In the case above, I would recommend the lady carry 15 pounds while her boyfriend lugs 50. Where togetherness isn't vital I urge people to travel at their own pace, the tortoises starting earlier and meeting the hares at the halfway point for lunch. I also advise people to savor the joys of solo travel or pick companions with similar capabilities. Increasingly on the trail I meet carefree groups of women happily poking along together, free of the strain of performing or keeping up with men.

The experts have learned some interesting facts that can help us walk more functionally. Walking involves about a hundred different muscles, but *all* the walker's propulsive thrust is delivered by the terminal bone of the big toe. Our computer propels us by converting potential energy to kinetic energy with almost 50% efficiency. Walking is a state of carefully controlled falling, using the acceleration of gravity for the purpose. There is an advantage, it turns out, to a certain amount of bobbing as we walk. The extra work of raising the body increases the help we get from gravity by permitting us to fall further with each step. Walking downhill is easier because the body can fall further. Freely swinging arms help walking efficiency by stabilizing the shoulders and pelvis with the thrust of their counter rotation.

Hurrying, especially uphill, can be counter productive in another way. Superexertion produces lactic acid in the blood, which hampers muscle performance, causes great discomfort and requires more than an hour for recovery, during which the walker suffers from exhaustion. So the clever backpacker's strategy requires keeping his activity level below the lactic acid formation stage. On difficult grades that means slowing the pace to a comfortable level or stopping frequently to rest and allow oxidation to flush the blood of acid buildup. By experimentation I have discovered that on the steepest trails under heavy load I drop below the level of painful lactic acid buildup by shortening each step from 18 inches to 14. That four inches makes a huge difference in my comfort.

It is important to react immediately to changes in grade. Failure to cut speed instantly when the trail turns abruptly upward places a demand on the body for extra exertion. And extra exertion consumes a disproportionately large part of one's store of energy. For instance, with the energy required to run fifty yards uphill one can easily hike a quarter mile up the same grade—in far greater comfort. Large expenditures of energy—running, lunging, jumping, taking huge steps, even hiking too fast—must be avoided.

On a really steep slope, at high altitude under load, or where the footing is bad (sand, scree or loose snow), I adjust my pace even more precisely by controlling my step-to-breath ratio. I may, for instance, take two steps to the breath, inhaling as I plant my right foot and exhaling as I plant my left. If that proves hard to maintain, I may slow to a breath for every step or even two breaths per step, with a greatly shortened stride. On exceptionally difficult slopes it is better to slow to a crawl, taking six inch steps, then to make the frequent stops a faster pace would require. Starting and stopping consume extra energy. A dependable rule of thumb is that where the going is hard it is better to slow down and keep going than it is to make frequent stops. An unlooked for dividend of step-to-breath counting is the welcome distraction the counting provides.

Daydream Painkiller

Every experienced backpacker at some time or other has experienced a sinking feeling when, coming around a bend, he discovers a long, shadeless trail switchbacking endlessly upward toward a high and distant pass. When I find myself faced with a prospect of this sort, I often distract myself from

daydream discomfort away

the ordeal with the self-induced euphoria that comes of concentrated daydreaming. In a state of mild self-hypnosis, my
daydreams so totally absorb my conscious mind that the discomfort of the grind goes mercifully dim.

As I start upward toward the pass I rummage about in my
memory for some event or scene that is so thoroughly pleasant
and engrossing that I recall it with consummate relish. Then I
unhurriedly embellish my recollection with the endless details
that enable it vividly to fill my conscious mind. At first, it may
be hard to escape into the past, but as the details pile up my
awareness of present time and distance almost ceases. I climb
automatically, sufficiently aware of my surroundings to make
the necessary adjustments, but too engrossed with my dream
to feel the discomfort. In fact, I'm sometimes reluctant, when
the pass has been reached, to abandon my dream and shift my
attention to the country ahead!

While I find daydreaming dependable and easily sustained,
some people prefer the more companionable distraction of
conversation. One of my regular walking companions, when
we face a demanding stretch of trail, will say "Well, what shall
we talk about?" We may very well get rid of a quarter of a mile
before we settle on a suitable topic. Often we trade accounts of
movies, dreams, books, trout we have caught or mountains we

rest stops are a vital part of walking.

have climbed. Sometimes we may be driven to simple word games (especially useful with children) like Twenty Questions or Animal-Mineral-Vegetable. If we have been out in the country awhile, we may get rid of half an hour concocting menus for fantastic meals. Talking as we move upward tends to slow the pace, but that, in turn, further reduces the discomfort.

The Art of Resting

Despite my advice "to slow down and keep going," rest stops are a vital part of walking. Unless the trail is like a sidewalk, one has little opportunity for looking around; the footing requires almost undivided attention. The walking itself is usually the least memorable part of any trip. So rest stops offer a means of savoring the country as well as restoring the body. One school holds that rests ought to be ruled by the clock, i.e. so many minutes of resting followed by so many minutes of hiking. This arbitrary arrangement makes no allowance for the difficulty of the terrain or the allure of the country.

But what's worse is the notion that one needs to be ruled by the clock, even in the wilderness. The tyranny of time, it seems to me, is one of the things that people go to the woods to escape. I am willing to admit the usefulness of a wristwatch in the woods for arranging a rendezvous with other watch-wearing members of the party—but I find clock time as dispensable in the wilds as doorbells, radios, telephones and cars, and I refuse to carry a watch, with only minor inconvenience.

Telling Time by Compass

If I really need to know the time my compass will give a rough approximation, provided the sun is shining. I set the compass in the sun, settle the needle on north, then set off the declination (17 degrees east in California). With the compass thus oriented, I stand a straight twig on the compass rim so that its shadow falls across the needle hub to the opposite rim. The position of the shadow on the opposite rim gives me a close approximation of sun time—by thinking of the compass as a watch with north at noon.

To reconcile sun time to daylight saving time, I add an hour. To tell time early or late in the day one only needs to know the hours of sunrise and sunset. Of course, some allowance must be made for mountains that rise high to either the east or west. Time is still important, but it is sun time, not clock time, that counts. How long before sunset, when it starts to grow cool? How long before dark? These are the pertinent questions in the wilds.

Getting back to rest stops, most walkers, provided they have a modicum of self-discipline and know how far they have to go, will find it more satisfactory to rest when they want to or need to. I like to stop, if I can manage it, beside a stream, at the top of a slope, in the first shade after a treeless stretch, where a log or rock forms a natural seat, or at any point where the view is unusually fine. I also favor mossy dells, waterfalls, brilliant patches of wildflowers, and fords where I can wash my feet or set up my rod and take a few casts.

When it comes to a real rest, I like to imagine I have earned it. On a particularly difficult slope, for instance, I might promise myself a rest after another hundred steps. Sometimes a hundred is impossible and I have to settle for fifty or even twenty-five. But if I get to thirty-five and think I can squeeze out another fifteen—I try it. For variety, and to add to the distraction, I sometimes count my steps backwards.

When I am ready to rest I take some pains to enjoy it. I slip out of my pack (leaving it propped against a rock or tree to make it easy to put back on) and sit or lie down. If my boots are the least bit uncomfortable or my feet are damp, I take off both boots and socks and set them to air in the sun or breeze. If there is water running nearby, I give my feet a soapless washing and rub and let them dry in the sun. If I am feeling faint or tired I lie down with my feet propped high against a tree so the blood can drain from my legs back into my body. Once my fatigue has drained away and my breathing has returned to normal, I usually have something to eat.

Sometimes the greatest benefit of a rest stop—especially if there are children along—is having some fun, doing a little exploring. I like to stroll away from the trail to have a look at country I would otherwise miss. Often enough, I discover something unsuspected—an abandoned prospect hole, a bed of mushrooms, a hidden view, the remains of a lean-to, a tiny spring or a wild sheep horn.

A rest may last anywhere from thirty seconds to overnight! When the time comes to move on, it is vital to start out at a moderate pace. There is a tendency, especially with children, to rocket up the trail after a refreshing rest. I have often seen eager children start off at a run, slow to a walk, then sink into a panting, dispirited trudge—all within sixty seconds.

The Hikers' Warmup

As anyone who's read a running book knows, it can be vital to loosen, stretch and warm-up your muscles before heavy exercise—like backpacking. The alternative can be stiffness, soreness, early fatigue and pulled muscles. The older you are or the colder it is, the more important it is to warm-up. I always stretch the backs of my legs (hamstrings) and Achilles tendons by bracing my hands against a tree or rock, straightening my body at a 45° angle to the ground and lowering my heels gently to the ground for a minute.

I find it equally beneficial and wonderfully stress relieving to loosen my muscles after hiking. When I shuck off my pack after a long haul I often feel stiff and weary—until five minutes of Yoga stretching on my foam pad rejuvinates and refreshes me. The transformation must be experienced to be believed. When ligaments and muscles are gently guided back into their natural state after prolonged effort, stiffness and fatigue simply dissolve. The single most rewarding exercise for me after hard hiking involves lying on my stomach, putting my hands in the push-up position, then, keeping my pelvis on the mat, gradually straightening my arms, throwing back my head and bending my spine backward, keeping my knees locked.

After several deep breaths, I turn my head as far as possible (until I can see my feet) on one side then the other. Then I relax my knees, lower my elbows to the pad and lie relaxed, back still bent, breathing deeply for another minute. Other stretches of great benefit after removing a pack include slowly rotating the neck, rotating the shoulders and rotating the ankles.

The "Limp" Step

The single most valuable (and spectacular) walking technique I know of, one which literally flushes away fatigue, is variously called the "rest step" or "limp step." Though little known among backpackers, this mountaineer's trick is based on the simplest of principles. When a hiker climbs steeply or carries great weights, the strain on the muscles around the knee is excessive and these muscles quickly fill with lactic and carbonic acids, the products of fatigue. This buildup of acids in overworked muscles, in turn, produces the painful ache that makes terrific slopes or heavy loads so uncomfortable.

The rest step is designed to flush away the acids of fatigue, thus relieving the ache they create. In the course of normal

Limp-stepping brings amazing relief:

walking knee muscles never quite relax. But if at some point in the step the leg is allowed to go entirely limp, even for only a fraction of a second, the excess acids are carried away and the pain miraculously disappears.

The necessary relaxation can be managed in either of two ways. The leading leg can be allowed to go limp for an instant just after the foot is placed for a new step and just before the weight is shifted to it. Or the trailing leg can be relaxed just after the weight is transferred to the lead leg and just before the trailing leg is lifted. I have gotten in the habit of relaxing the lead leg, but most people seem to find it easier to let the trailing leg go limp. The trailing leg method is also easier to learn and easier to teach. My daughter learned it when she was eight.

We were day hiking up a relentlessly climbing trail that gains 1200 feet in less than a mile. When she complained that she was tired and her legs hurt, I had her stop and shift all her weight first to one leg then the other, explaining that the pain would go away from a leg allowed to go limp. After she had stopped to flush her legs in this manner several times, I suggested that she take a small step forward with the leg that was relaxed, explaining that it was less tiring to keep going, even very slowly, when you rested your legs. Before we reached the top she was able to flush the fatigue from her legs whenever she needed to, without stopping.

As few as two or three limp steps in succession will usually bring amazing relief. Of course, the acids of fatigue continue to collect as long as the knees continue to work hard, so it soon becomes necessary to flush them again. But I find that after half a dozen limp steps I can return to my normal stride for anywhere from ten to a hundred yards. Besides offering relief from aching muscles, limp-stepping also provides comic relief by causing its practitioners to look a little like staggering drunks.

The "Indian" Step

A technique of somewhat narrower application is the Indian Step, a style of walking long used by cross-country skiers and European gymnasts as well as American Indians. Modern Americans tend to walk without swinging their hips. The Indian travels more efficiently. At the end of each step he swings the hip forward as well as the leg, pivoting at the waist. And he leans forward slightly as he walks. This forward lean and turning of the hips lengthens the stride, positions the feet almost directly in front of one another, and minimizes the wasteful up and down movement. The result is a more fluid, floating walk, with less wasted motion. And on easy ground the longer stride produces more speed. The chief disadvantages of the Indian Step are that it is difficult to master, requiring agility and balance; and the advantages are greatest for the unburdened walker.

I occasionally use the Indian Step if I am lightly burdened and wish to travel rapidly across level terrain that offers good footing. The easiest way to get the feel of the step is consciously to stretch the stride, thrusting the hip forward, aiming the foot for the center of the trail, swinging the shoulders counter to the hip thrust. Once the rhythm is established the shoulder swing can be reduced. Walking on narrow city curbs is a good way to practice.

Having dealt with uphill and level trail hiking, it is time to go down. It is common to feel relief when the trail starts down because it is so much easier on the lungs. But downhill travel is twice as hard on the legs as going up. When descending a steep trail I try to cushion the shock of each downward step by rolling my hip forward (not unlike the Indian Step movement) and placing my foot with the knee slightly bent. As I transfer my weight I allow my knee to flex so that it functions in much the same fashion as an automobile shock absorber, reducing the jarring that downhill travel inevitably produces.

Trails provide a measure of dependability and security. Cross-country walking is altogether different. Instead of relying on an established course, one must find his own way; instead of the improved footing of a prepared trail, there are obstacles to contend with. Carrying a pack cross-country can be serious business and requires much greater experience, balance, strength, adventurousness and caution than does backpacking by trail.

In the space of a mile, one may have to contend with brush, bog, loose sand, boulder slopes, snow, deadfalls, mud, streams and cliffs. And one of the most treacherous steep slopes I ever descended was covered with innocent-looking tufts of extremely slippery grass. Just as slippery are glacially polished slabs that are wet, mossy or invisibly dusted with sand. Footing of this sort demands caution. I often take some trouble to climb around a wet or mossy slab, and when traction is vital I test the slope for sand by listening for the telltale grating sound. When I must cross slippery terrain, I often twist my foot slightly as I put my weight upon it to determine how well my boot soles are gripping.

When climbing a sandy slope it is important to plant the foot as flatly as possible; the greater the surface area of boot on sand the shorter the distance one is likely to slip backward. If there are rocks or patches of grass or low brush, I think of them as stepping stones and zig-zag from one to the other. Sometimes steep sand is best treated like snow and the easiest way up is a series of switchbacking traverses or a herringbone step in which the toes are turned outward.

Crossing Spring Snow

Hard and hummocky slopes of spring snow can be extremely tiring, and nothing short of wading tests the waterproofing of boots so severely. It is virtually impossible to keep feet dry. All one can do is carry several pairs of dry socks for a single day's travel. If I am rushing the season, I content myself with day hikes and keep dry boots waiting at the trailhead.

In the spring there is the constant danger of falling through a thin crust of snow with painful, even serious, results. There is hardly an easier way to bark shins, twist ankles and even break legs. The margins of spring snowfields should always be treated with suspicion. So should snow-covered logs and snow from which issues the muffled sound of gurgling water. The best strategy I know for testing suspect snow is to kick it

spring snow by a rock is often undermined....

so step over such areas.

without actually committing any weight to it. If it withstands the kicking it can probably support my weight. Sometimes a big step or jump will avoid the necessity of stepping on what looks like rotten or undermined snow.

In the spring it can be dangerous to ford creeks and streams, never mind rivers. If you can't find a log or a series of stepping stones, you'll have to wade. The first decision is whether to protect your feet but soak your boots, or take a chance on injuring your feet (and increasing the likelihood of falling) by going barefoot. If you choose the latter, be sure your socks and boots are tied securely to your pack or around your neck as you wade, so that they can't possibly be lost if you fall or go under—unless you're prepared to walk barefoot to the car! When wearing a pack on a dangerous crossing, always release the hipbelt and loosen the shoulder straps so you can jettison it instantly to protect yourself from drowning.

Fording Streams

If conditions warrant, send the strongest man in the party across first with a rope but no pack. A fixed rope tied tightly between trees will provide security and peace of mind. So will a staff to probe for holes and brace like a third leg against the current. Choose a wide shallow ford over a short but swift or deep one. The job will be easier if you start on the upstream side of a good fording site and plan to angle downstream, because that's where you'll end up anyway. If you can help it, don't cross immediately above a falls, cataract or other substantial hazard. Organize your party for the safest possible crossing. And remember that risks are enormously magnified when you're traveling alone. It's better to change your plans or make any detour than it is to take a chance when there's no one to help if you get in trouble.

Nothing consumes energy in such big gulps as maneuvers that require extra effort, like taking a giant step up onto a rock

the arms can help on a long step up.

or log. If I cannot easily make my way around such obstacles, I transfer most of the extra effort to my shoulders and arms by placing both hands on top of the knee that is making the step and pushing down hard as I step upward.

On exceptionally steep rocky slopes, it sometimes becomes necessary to step forward onto the toe of the foot instead of the heel. Toe stepping adds power and balance on steep grades, but soon tires calf muscles. It helps to alternate heel and toe steps to prevent the cramping the latter produce. By following ten toe steps with twenty heel steps, I spread the work over two sets of muscles. The necessity of counting helps distract me from the rigours of the climb. If this arrangement continues to produce excessive fatigue, I sheer off from the fall-line and climb in longer but easier switchbacking traverses.

When climbing cross-country it is sometimes necessary to remind oneself that the easiest route up may not be the easiest way down. Going up, I generally go out of my way to avoid sand, snow and scree; but coming down I go out of my way to make use of them. Nothing is so pleasant after a hard climb up a mountain as glissading down a slanting snowfield or gliding with giant, sliding steps down slopes of sand or gravel.

Rules for New Climbers

Scrambling—climbing that requires the use of hands, but not ropes—demands agility, good balance, endurance and desire. Success may depend on the scrambler's ability to discover a feasible route by studying the slope during the approach and by consulting a large scale topographic map. The basic rules for beginning climbers include: never climb alone; never go up a pitch you cannot get down; never climb on your knees; lean out from, not in toward the slope when exposure is great; and never take chances or attempt maneuvers that are beyond your skill.

Despite the need for caution, climbing can be enjoyed by most walkers, including women and children. Both my wife and daughter have climbed a number of peaks with me; my daughter made her first ascent when she was six. It is unfortunate that so many people think climbing means inching up sheer cliffs by means of ropes, pitons and limitless willpower. There is immense satisfaction to be gained in scrambling up peaks that demand little more than determination and offer no disconcerting exposure.

Climbing can be as safe as the climber cares to make it. As I come down a mountain late in the day, I remind myself that the majority of mountaineering accidents occur after three in the afternoon, and that twice as many falls happen on the way down as on the way up. Expert climbers force themselves to descend with caution, thinking out difficult steps in advance to keep down the chance of injury.

Rock-hopping—crossing a boulder field by stepping or jumping from rock to rock—is probably the most demanding and dangerous way to travel in the mountains, but it is often unavoidable. I mentally try to keep a step ahead of my feet so when I run out of rocks I will be able to stop. I also treat every boulder, no matter how large, as though the addition of my weight will cause it to move. To slow myself down on a dangerous slope, I sometimes think back to a cross-country backpacking descent on which a companion, when forced to leap from a rolling boulder, opened six inches of his leg to the bone. Whenever I am forced to make a sudden or awkward jump, I try to land simultaneously on both feet with knees bent, to cushion the shock and minimize the danger of injury.

Getting Off the Trail

A majority of hikers, or so it seems to me, are slaves to the trails. Many newcomers to walking are perhaps not aware that trails are the means, not the ends. The trail, however faint, is merely an extension of civilization. Wilderness does not begin until the trail is left behind. Many trip planners, without thinking, plot their routes exclusively from existing trail systems. And many squander a whole vacation on wilderness travel that never leaves the beaten path. But the solitude—the true wilderness experience—does not materialize until the traveler is finding his own way through wild country, rather than following a route marked by others.

By far the easiest way to escape the trail is to day hike, carrying only sweater, lunch and first aid kit. More country can be covered in a day without pack than on a weekend under load. Hikers who want to spend a maximum amount of time in truly wild country may find it more fruitful to car camp close to the trailhead and spend the time dayhiking. I sometimes

"Getting to the top" can be a joy.

begin a wilderness weekend by backpacking cross-country for less than a mile to some unsuspected campsite by a spring or small creek; I then spend the bulk of my time dayhiking unencumbered.

A good many trips have been ruined in the planning by the seemingly harmless assumption: "We ought to be able to make ten miles a day." On some days fifty feet would be too far. People have a habit of committing themselves to rigid goals: making 11.2 miles, fishing Lockjaw Lake, climbing Indian Peak. Somehow these achievements become substituted for the original or underlying reason for going—to enjoy roaming wild country. When people become so achievement oriented that they measure the success of a trip in terms of miles tramped, elevation gained or speed records, they often find themselves losing interest in wilderness travel. Working toward ambitious goals becomes too much like the rat-race at home.

One of the greatest sources of joy I know is climbing to some attractive summit. It has been a long time since I called myself a mountain climber, but I enjoy getting to the top as much as ever. And I get just as much pleasure from walking up a little granite dome after dinner to watch the sun go down as I do spending all day working my way up a big mountain. The important thing to remember is that anyone can (and should) make his or her way to the top of an appropriate hill, ridge or peak. I know of no better way to savor the wilderness.

Blending Into the Country

When I was a boy I had the good fortune to belong to a small group led by the well-known author-naturalist, Vinson Brown. Vince used to take us into wild places he knew in the hills and station us, out of sight of one another, perhaps a hundred feet apart, on conveniently located rocks and logs. After wiggling into comfortable positions, we would be instructed to sit absolutely still for five minutes, not moving anything but our eyes.

If we were quiet enough, Vince told us, the birds and insects and small animals in the area would come gradually to accept us as part of the environment, just as they accepted the rocks or logs on which we were sitting. It was truly remarkable how well it worked. I don't know a better way to get close to the country, and often when I am walking alone in wild country I will seat myself in some fruitful looking place and let myself once again become part of the country.

Trail Manners

With more and more people walking in the wilds, trail manners have become more important. In most states discharging firearms, even during hunting season, is illegal across or in the vicinity of a trail. Equally objectionable is the boom of gunfire which invades privacy and solitude, and shatters the wilderness experience of other travelers for miles around. Guns are not needed as protection against wildlife and they have no place in today's crowded wildlands.

Horses and pack stock, once necessary to reach remote country, are now less common. But since stock can be unpredictable and difficult to control, it retains the right-of-way on trails. Walkers should move several yards off the trail, preferably downslope, and stand quietly while animals pass. Since walkers inevitably travel at different speeds, slower-moving parties should be considerate enough of faster walkers to let them move by. And fast hikers ought to politely ask permission to pass when the trail is narrow.

Over-riding the backpacker's concern for his comfort should be a sense of responsibility toward the country through which he passes. Increased travel in diminishing wild areas makes it necessary for all of us, consciously, to protect the environment and keep it clean. On the trail this means throwing away nothing, not even a cigarette butt, broken shoelace or match. In camp it means burning, then bagging, but never burying, garbage. Leftover edibles, not including egg shells and orange peels, can be scattered for the birds and animals. Everything else should go in heavy plastic garbage bags to be packed out. The thoughtful walker takes pride in leaving no trace of his passing.

Family Trips

Many parents who badly want their kids to love the wilds either cram it down their throats or fail to make those first trips really memorable. To ensure that your children enjoy a happy outing means tailoring it in all aspects to maximize their enjoyment. The same goes for other strangers to the wilds, whether girlfriends, children, parents, brides, or even inexperienced friends.

Generally speaking, I feel parents should not take their children backpacking until: (1) they themselves can travel in the wilds with some degree of comfort and competence; (2) the children have been taken on several successful day hikes; (3) parents are willing to tailor an overnight trip to

Kids are good at finding firewood...
...and mud!

Kids love tube tents

country they know, expressly for the pleasure of their children; (4) the children want (or are at least willing) to go; and (5) the parents genuinely want them along. Families able to meet these criteria have a fighting chance for a pleasant trip.

The most common cause of disastrous family trips, it seems to me, is the failure of parents to see the trip through their children's eyes. Any child will ask "If it isn't fun, why do it?" He does not insist every minute be fun, but he will expect that, taken as a whole, the trip should be pleasant. After all, what good is a vacation if it isn't fun? The honest adult will find it hard to object to such logic.

Food that meets the adult backpacker's demands may or may not satisfy your children. Special emphasis should be put on snack foods and liquids. To maintain energy and prevent dehydration, children will need plenty of both. To encourage the between meal eating so necessary in the wilds, plenty of goodies are needed, especially gorp, cheese, salami, nuts and dried fruit. Children should be urged to drink small amounts of water often while traveling, and quantities of lemonade, Koolaid, Fizzies and reconstituted milk should be available in camp. Since kids will immediately notice that camp milk tastes "funny," powdered flavorings should be carried to transform it into chocolate milk, cocoa and milkshakes.

Getting Kids up the Trail

When the trailhead has been reached and the loads handed out, the real work begins. Getting children up the trail and into camp demands patience, a strong back and considerable psychology. Parents unwilling or unable to keep the children amused and moving—without losing their own sense of humor—will wish they had left them home. So will the children! Without supervision, children tend to start out fast, which means they will soon want to rest. It is hard to curb the enthusiasm and effervescence that eats up their energy without curtailing the fun of the trip; it is also hard to keep them going when they feel tired and want to rest; and children fatigue quickly.

It is unfair to expect children to have the self-discipline necessary to conserve energy for the climb ahead. Instead, one has to supply incentives, distractions, goals and just plain entertainment—with the minimum necessary discipline mixed in.

Call the trip a "walk," "walking" is fun but "hiking" is work. Making the trip a lark for the kids means getting into the spirit of *their* adventure rather than fretting about the slowness of the pace. Keep children moving but don't try to make them hurry; it will only slow them down and rob them of their cheerfulness. Make sure they get away from the trail occasionally. Let them put down their packs and go investigate something they've discovered.

Take them off the trail to see mossy glens, snowbanks, waterfalls, a tree that looks like a witch. If they've been trudging along wearily for awhile, don't wait for them to ask for a rest or simply sit down. Stop voluntarily, give them something to eat and show them something interesting. If they're happy they'll recover from their fatigue with amazing swiftness. Keep in mind the fact that the long range goal is not just to get them to the camp before lunch—it's to make the trip so much fun that they'll want to come again.

It's always a good idea to keep watch on childrens' feet. By putting a stop to chafing in the early stages you may avoid having to carry a child to the car! I have more than once discovered my daughter hiking happily along despite the fact that one sock had worked so far down her foot that it had disappeared entirely into her boot. Fortunately, children's feet take the abuse of rough country much better than their parents' and do not easily blister.

I find it important on the trail to talk to children a good part of the time. I give them progress reports "We're more than halfway ... It's only fifteen minutes until lunch ... There's a spring where we can get a drink behind that big tree ... It's all downhill to camp." Whenever I can, I praise their achievements. I try to distract them from the drudgery of the trail, and in doing so I find I have distracted myself.

When they grow weary of such temporal phenomena as birds' nests, rills and rock rabbits, I try to stir their imagination by pointing out a cloud formation that looks like a ship, a leaning tree that resembles a poised runner or a patch of lichen that looks like a lion. Finding strange likenesses can be made into a contest in which children point out their own discoveries. The reward for the most imaginative can be a specially prized piece of candy.

I carry a considerable stock of snacks in a wide variety, and I keep them concealed to add mystery and anticipation. It's less important that kids eat well at mealtime than it is to feed them snacks between meals to keep their energy and spirits up. I pass out food with the smallest provocation and often with none at all.

Motivating Little Hikers

It's always important to keep the kids happy, but there's still the problem of getting them up the trail. A minimal amount of discipline, and self-discipline, is indispensable. So is a certain amount of desire on the child's part to please his parents and do his part. I explain at the outset that while we're going to stop and rest, play games, explore and generally have fun, we still have to make it to camp before lunch, so we'll have time to set up camp and spend the afternoon playing without our packs. And that means we have to keep moving. As we move along, I show kids easier ways to get around obstacles, help foot draggers, readjust packs, show how the Indians walk, and if the trail grows steep, I demonstrate the rest step, which I represent variously as the "polar bear shuffle," "kangaroo limp," "dromedary drag," etc.

If there are several children, I work most with the slowest ones. Sometimes the slowest becomes the fastest if you put them in the lead, explaining that they now have the responsibility for keeping the group on the trail, showing them how to recognize blazes and ducks and the footworn groove. It is usually best to bring up the rear when hiking with children, so you can help the ones who fall behind and so you'll know if a child quietly sits down on a rock or wanders off while the rest of the party marches by.

The hardest part of handling a group of kids is keeping them together and controlling the rest stops. Energetic older boys will want to keep going while younger girls will fre-

introduce your kids
to the wilds...

quently want to rest. It's not difficult to spread your party all over the mountain. I urge the stoppers to keep going, and as a last resort I take their packs. If other kids get too far ahead, I may saddle them with the unwanted packs. When we stop for a rest I encourage the energetic ones to explore the immediate area while the tired ones sit and puff.

When the weariest seem to be somewhat restored, I simultaneously announce we must be off and pass out lemondrops all around. It is important after a rest not to let children dash up the trail with recharged enthusiasm or they'll burn themselves out after only a few yards and plead for another rest. If they fail to restrain themselves, after you've explained the reason for starting off slowly, there is nothing to do but nag. Chronic fast starters are best reminded at the end of the rest instead of after they take off.

Family Camping Strategy

Even with all these stratagems, the trail can become monotonous, and when the group becomes dull or dispirited I call an early rest. Everyone takes off his pack and we make a little side trip to some interesting spot out of sight of the trail—usually a waterfall or a cool glade or a lookout point, and we have a drink of lemonade (powder and plastic bottle must be handy) or lie in the cool grass, or throw snowballs off the cliff. This side trip is likely to refresh the group and the time spent seems a worthwhile investment. Progress, in this fashion, will be anywhere from a quarter mile to one mile per hour.

When camp is reached (and by now it should be evident why it needs to be close and the trail well known) some kids will want to flop down and rest, others will want to explore. No one will want to unpack, lay out beds or gather wood. The best strategy is to let everyone squander at least half an hour before assigning chores. Everyone should have something to do; if the tasks are thoughtfully assigned and described, previously exhausted children will go to work with surprising enthusiasm.

Limit the amount that thirsty children drink, but allow them—in fact urge them—to drink frequently from unpolluted streams and rills and your water bottle or canteen. Snowball fights and singing make good diversions. So do yodeling and echoing. Give kids the sense of helping you and finding the way. Don't communicate anxiety about reaching camp, snakes, storms, or mosquitos. You must be relaxed and at home in the woods if you want your children to feel the same way. Don't panic if they step near the edge of a cliff; their natural caution should protect them. Don't yell at them. Be

don't panic
at every danger...

alert for excessive fatigue, dizziness, blisters, chafing clothes, sunburn and chapped lips.

Explain in advance that you want to keep them comfortable and therefore they must let you know what's bothering them. They'll tell you all right! When you come to sand on smooth slab, wet slippery surfaces, loose gravel, mud, etc., calmly demonstrate how to cross safely. Celebrate all achievement; be liberal with praise and rewards. Teach your kids not to litter and get them to help you pick up gum wrappers and trash—if the going is not too difficult—to be deposited in one of your spare plastic bags.

Toilet Training

Impress your kids that nothing must be left behind to mar the wilderness, especially used toilet paper! Children at all times should carry about three feet of TP folded up in a pocket. Teach them when traveling to choose a place that won't be found; supervise if necessary. Show them how to fold the used paper inward for easy handling and put it in a plastic bag for later burning. In camp, build a latrine and furnish it with TP and a collection bag for used paper. Unless you provide instruction there are sure to be toilet paper streamers decorating the trees, and the responsibility will be yours.

It's a poor idea to plan to take children cross-country in rough terrain unless they are large, strong, proven hikers. Being closer to the ground, children see relatively small objects as real obstacles. A rock that's just a knee-high step to you will be a waist-high roadblock to a six-year-old; a good scramble for you may be a nightmare for them. Forget boulder-hopping altogether.

In camp, find them rocks to climb, rills to dam, a snowpatch to slide on; define the bathroom area boundaries, explain camp rules regarding fire, food, muddy feet in the tent and the sanctity of the kitchen during meal preparation. Alert them to

family camping means carrying a little more.

the continued need for wood and water. Explain that, like Indians, you plan to leave this camp so no one will know you've been there.

Taking children in to the wilderness can be demanding, even maddening, but by allowing yourself to see the trip through their eyes you can share their wonder, joy and adventure. You can remember what it feels like to be a kid in the woods when everything is new and mysterious and exciting. And when the trip is over and you're homeward bound there is deep satisfaction in hearing your youngest ask "Daddy, when can we go again?"

Boots & Packs

Your walking success will depend greatly on the footwear you chose to bring along. Hopefully your boots (or running shoes or sandals or tennis shoes, etc.) are comfortable, supportive and well broken in. Since footwear and foot care belong together, I've put both in the next chapter, *Keeping Fit*. There's been a revolution in footwear in the past few years. If you're still carrying big, stiff, heavy leather boots for use on not-too-difficult terrain, you might want to read about the new, light, flexible boots in my *Pleasure Packing for the 80's* before planning your next trip.

It's hard to overemphasize the importance of boot weight. It's well known that a pound on the feet is equivalent to five on the back, but think what that means on a ten mile walk. If you take an average 2000 steps per mile, it means you lift five tons in ten miles for every pound of boot on your feet! So every pound you save—going from four to three pound boots, or three pound boots to the new two pounders—saves the energy needed to lift five tons. Think what that energy saving could mean to your enjoyment of a trip, or how it might extend your range? Instead of collapsing in camp to soak and patch your swollen red feet you might actually enjoy a stroll after supper.

I also hope you brought the right pack, something sturdy, comfortable, and appropriate to the size of your load—since you're stuck with it for the rest of the trip. If your pack is un-satisfactory, resolve to bring something better on your next trip. If you wince at every step, or the pack pulls back on you, consider the many cunning new designs I discuss in *Pleasure Packing*. If you've got a terraplane, you may wish you had more hip support. If you're bushwhacking (cross-country) you may wish you'd brought an internal framed pack that has a lower center of gravity, moves with you and doesn't throw you off balance or get caught on branches as often as your

Carry only what
you really need...

external frame pack. If your load is moderate but the pack is trying to throw you on your back, the center of your load may be too far from your back. A good pack bag keeps the weight within nine inches of the frame. Or you may be one of the many who's discovering the "pull-back" characteristic of wraparound packs.

Blister Prevention

Maybe, if you're uncomfortable, you can solve the problem with adjustments. If something's gouging you in the back, stop and repack. Now! Maybe you need to tighten the backbands or webbing. Maybe all you need is to shift the weight from your shoulders to the hipbelt. If your pack hasn't a hipbelt or you can't easily transfer all pack weight to the one you have, resolve to come better equipped next trip. Sometimes you need to rehang the shoulder straps (assuming yours are adjustable). Often the problem is even easier to solve.

Is there a fold in your shirt or sweater underneath the shoulder strap? Is the hipbelt making the belt buckle beneath it dig into your waist? Make sure you minimize chafing by paying close attention to all the points at which your body bears weight or there's friction of any kind. The lightest rubbing, if it continues mile after mile, can produce pain, irritation, blisters or loss of skin that can become disabling. Maybe the irritation is slight at first so you procrastinate. But ask yourself: How will I hike tomorrow if I let a blister develop today?

Sometimes one shoulder strap is a tad tighter than the other. After an hour or so, this faint imbalance can result in an aching shoulder or neck or back. To insure maximum comfort at the end of the day (when you're sure to be tired anyway) be sensitive to the smallest discomfort. Then stop and do something about it RIGHT NOW. Veteran hikers baby themselves because they know what's coming if they don't. It's a sign of inexperience to hobble up the trail enduring discomfort or suffering from yesterday's neglect. Concentrate on your problem and you'll discover your pack and clothing is more adjustable than you imagined. Experiment and you'll find ways to increase your walking comfort. And do it before your tender city skin turns pink.

Once blisters have formed the problem is quadrupled, because chances are good you can't totally prevent friction on the damaged area. And continued rubbing on blistered areas can mean real suffering. What if your feet hurt so much you can't put on your boots or can't walk back to the car? How do you carry your pack if your hips or shoulders are raw? Once the skin is damaged you're stuck. It won't fully heal while you wait, unless you can lay around camp for a week. Prevention is the only solution to the problem of injured tissue on any part of the body. For the backpacker, whose life may depend on maintaining good health, an ounce of injury prevention may be worth a ton of cure.

Sometimes chafing can be lessened by improvising padding inside the shoulder straps or hipbelt with a carefully folded bandana or t-shirt. And make a note to make this temporary measure permanent before your next trip. Hipbelt padding, once optional, should be regarded as essential for comfortably carrying the entire load when you want to rest your shoulders. Nylon line "clothes hangers" are also valuable if you want to air out the socks you just took off, stow a sweater that won't fit in the pack or dry your laundry. Tie *everything* on, no matter how secure you think those spare socks are tucked in. Don't wait until you've lost some vital item of clothing (it's vital if you brought it) because you're too lazy to tie it on.

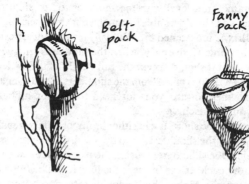

Belt-pack

Fanny-pack

If Your Pack Bag Rips

If your pack bag rips or bursts you shouldn't be in trouble—as long as you have a ground cloth or tent and some nylon line. Simply fold your tarp into a big rectangle and position all your gear in a neat heap, with the heaviest items on top. Then fold the sides in and flop your bundle onto the bare frame, so the edges are all inside. Then lash it to the frame securely and continue on your way with a pack that's probably closer to your body than before. Remember, do all you can to minimize pack depth. Put heaviest items closest to your body, hold pack depth to nine inches, and never put anything but featherweight items in that pocket on the back of your pack. If you get tired of taking off your pack everytime you want to get something out of its pockets, resolve to try a belt pouch or small fanny pack worn in front next trip. All can be marvelously handy on the trail for carrying small items and even handier on day hikes or climbs from base camp on layover days. Bulging pockets are no aid to comfort, and lifting a pocketful of knives and gadgets with every step uses energy to no purpose.

In a properly fitting loaded pack, the shoulder straps should meet the frame on a level with the shoulder top or slightly above it, and you should be able to hunch your shoulders high enough to lift the unfastened hipbelt easily into the ideal position for tightening. Conversely, when the hipbelt is snugged moderately tight it should accept the full weight of the loaded pack when all weight is taken from the shoulders. Bend over as you lift one knee toward your forehead to test for hipbelt pinch on your stomach.

If the frame is too short, it will either be impossible to get all of the weight off the shoulders, or to do so will drop the crossbar well below the shoulders, causing the pack to ride low and away from the back. If the frame is too long it will be impossible to fasten the hipbelt high enough to support weight unless the shoulder straps are abnormally tight.

Tips on Packing Up

Sometimes pack discomfort is due solely to carrying too much or too many heavy items. My procedure, once my partner and I have decided what to take, may be helpful. First we spread out all the food and community gear on an old tarp. Then one of us divides it on the basis of both weight and bulk into two equal stacks. I don't bother with a scale. Hefting an item in each hand at arms' length lets me make the piles sufficiently equal in weight. After one of us divides the gear, the other gets first choice of piles. Sometimes one man, because of his pack size, will be short on space and may request less bulky items, but we still split the weight evenly, unless there is a marked difference in body size. Carrying ability is proportional to body weight. Your performance will be seriously impaired, say the physiologists, if you try to carry a pack weighing more than 20-25% of your body weight.

After combining my share of the community gear with my personal equipment, I make up my pack. First I set aside clothing that may be needed in a hurry, trail food, notebook, pencil, compass, first aid kit, camera, lip salve, sunburn cream, bandana, mosquito dope and anything else I expect to need on the trip. Then, I make a layer of the heaviest, densest items in such a way that the weight will lie as high and as close to my back as possible. From the remaining gear I take those items least likely to be needed and, working my way to the top, fill the remainder of the pack snugly. If I am hiking in shorts, my long trousers are packed on top for easy access, or in the lower compartment of a divided bag.

The gear set aside to be used on the trail is then systematically divided between the pack's outside pockets. To find things fast, it helps to use the same arrangement for every trip. For instance, although I sprinkle wooden kitchen matches in every pocket, the main (camp) supply always rides in the upper right hand pocket. With the last of the small items stowed, I stuff my rolled foam mattress into (or onto) the top of the back pack and cinch down the flap over it. My sleeping bag is then strapped or snapped beneath the three quarter pack bag. Last to be attached is my two-piece fly rod, broken down, but with the reel still attached. The butt ends seat in a 35 mm film can taped to the bottom right rail. A thong at the top crossbar lashes the rod to the rail. Finally, I check all zippers, buttons, ties and lashings.

After taking a quick inventory of my pockets for necessities I slip into my pack and adjust the buckles so the weight is bourne equally by my shoulders and hips. With nothing further to detain me, I set forth up the trail.

STARTING OFF

Awakened in the dark
by the purling of Robins
I set myself deeper
in the frost stiff bag
and sink into sleep
as the day takes hold.

With new melted ice
from a rock bound pool
we wash back the night
from our cobwebbed faces
and breakfast on apples
from my father's farm.

As the sun breaks free
from the shadowed trees
and the stillness gives way
to the clamor of day
we gather our gear
and make ready to go.

Then with tentative steps
under unaccustomed loads
we set forth out the trail
in the growing light
through the warming air
on the first long trip
of the new found summer.

TWO
Keeping Fit

*Your Body's Needs... Exposure Dangers...
How to Stay Cool... Vapor Barrier Magic...
Make Yourself a VB Vest... Make Your Clothes
Work... Clothing Critique... Boots... Socks...
Foot Care Tips... Solo Travel Precautions...
Treating Shock & Bleeding... Dealing with
Sprains... Snakebite... Sunburn vs. Tan...
Beware Sunglasses... Altitude Sickness...
Hypothermia*

To know how to stay comfortable, warm and fit with the clothing you brought along, you first need to understand that highly sensitive organism, the human body. You must meet its basic needs or pain will swiftly follow. The body wants air temperature at the skin to be about 75°F, ranging from 72°F in the hands and feet to about 78°F in the head and trunk. Take away body heat faster than it's generated and the body turns dramatically defensive. To protect crucial head and trunk temperatures it swiftly cuts down blood circulation to the skin by constricting capillaries. If cooling continues, it severely shuts down blood flow to the arms and legs, chilling hands and feet. By allowing skin temperature to drop 20 degrees and reducing blood circulation to the feet by up to 95%, the body can cut overall heat losses by a startling 75%. When the body is threatened it doesn's fool around!

The body's thermostat is located in the chest area. If you chill the chest while trying to vent excess heat, you're liable to trigger the production (and resultant energy loss) of massive amounts of heat and moisture. So if you want to cool off without threatening the body, keep your front zippers closed and rely on venting at the shirttails, neck, cuffs—and armpits if your garments have underarm zippers.

The head is the only part of the body in which the capillaries do not contract, because the body knows survival depends on continued alert functioning of the brain. So when your skin turns cool and your hands and feet grow cold, pay attention. The body is trying to warn you that heat production can't keep up with heat loss. No mittens in the world will keep your hands warm if the body believes trunk temperature is threatened. So if your feet get cold, put on a hat and jacket— especially when sleeping with the head exposed.

Your Body's Needs

Almost as important to the body as maintaining an average 75°F temperature is the maintenance of moist—but not wet —skin. Comfort, to the body, is a surprisingly high relative humidity of 70-95%, despite the mind's belief that comfort means dry skin. This isn't the contradiction it seems. What the mind calls dry skin, really isn't. Truly dry skin quickly turns chapped, stiff, cracked and flaky. Open sores and bleeding follow. Properly moist, humid skin, on the other hand, isn't wet, either. What the body wants is a quarter inch thick cushioning layer of moist warm air, like an invisible second skin, shielding and lubricating but not wetting the skin. Humor the body by providing 70°F air with a normal 50% relative humidity, and it will easily maintain this suit of

invisible armor with as little as a pint of water a day. Destroy
this protective layer by exposure to a harsh environment and
the body goes wild in an effort to restore it. Sweat glands open
wide and the body goes all out to pump heated water vapor
through the skin. Until the layer is rebuilt, heat and water loss
from the body will be a terrific 6-800% above normal—
though at the time the mind may notice nothing because
evaporation is immediate. But after hiking in dry or cold air
for several hours you'll suddenly discover an insatiable thirst.
Your body is signaling dehydration and demanding
replacement of water—by the quart!

When the skin is below 75°F water vapor passes off unnoticed as "insensible perspiration"—after doing its job;
keeping the skin moist. But when skin temperature climbs
much above 75°F the body reacts to what it considers uncomfortable overheating by opening the sweat glands wider and
pouring out heated water to wet the skin with what we regard
distastefully as sweat. So in reality there are two kinds of
sweat: the one you don't feel or see that keeps your skin comfortably moist and alive, and the wet one produced by overheating.

The colder the air the less water it can hold. From the
body's standpoint winter ski touring conditions are as dry as
those in the desert: it's a struggle to get enough water. At 30°F
the relative humidity on bare skin is an arid 15%—even
though there's nothing but frozen water (snow) in sight! And
liquid water can be just as hard to come by as in the desert.
The body may need a gallon a day!

Though dry air sucks up ample moisture (and with its body
heat), the two greatest threats to body heat are wind (convection) and water (conduction) because each has the capacity to
swiftly obliterate that layer of moist warm air that shields the
body. Water's great conductivity—20 times that of still dry
air—instantly destroys the air layer and enormous heat loss
follows. Ten minutes exposure of the body to a 34°F water (if
you fall through thin winter ice on the pond) means likely

death by freezing! But the water doesn't have to be frigid to chill you. Air temperature of 68°F in a heated home is comfortably warm, but the same 68°F in a swimming pool water feels freezing. Why? In the house the body easily maintains its cushion of moist 75°F air. In the water it can't and the sudden 7° drop on bare skin is a shock.

Exposure Dangers

Slicing it even finer, if you work up a sweat jogging and return to that 68°F house after you've cooled down, the dampness of your clothes and skin produces chilling evaporative heat loss that will make the house seem chilly, no matter what else you do. But take a shower and put on dry clothes and presto! the 68°F house is warm again.

Wind chill may be even more threatening to the exposed body because the danger is less evident. Most deaths from hypothermia (brain and body core chilling) occur in deceptively mild (above freezing) air temperatures which have been drastically lowered (in chilling effect) because wind has blown away the body's protective layer of still, warm air, permitting rapid heat loss by convection. And it doesn't take much wind. On a 30°F day with a mild 10 mph wind, the effective air temperature on bare skin is a chilly 16°F. If the

avoid chilling...

wind freshens to a moderate 25 mph, the effective temperature drops to zero. And on a zero winter day a 30 mph wind is equivalent to a dangerous 50°F below on bare skin!

Combine the threats of wind and water and you multiply the danger by adding the terrible cooling power of evaporation. Exposed wet skin loses heat more than 200 times as fast as dry protected skin! Stand wet and naked in the wind after a swim on a cool summer day and you'll experience severe chilling in a matter of seconds. Even after you dry and dress it will take a long time to get warm. Sweat up your sleeping bag on a warm autumn evening and you're headed for trouble in the cool before dawn.

Though few campers are aware of it, it isn't uncommon for the weight of your sleeping bag to mysteriously jump 1½ to 2½ pounds in the space of a single summer night from accumulated condensed water vapor given off by the sleeping body.

How to Stay Cool

But the cooling effect of evaporation can be put to work in warm climates. Soak your hat and shirt (or everything but your boots) everytime you pass a stream, for blessed relief. If water is scarce, take advantage of what's known about blood circulation to the head and neck. Veteran desert travelers know the most effective use of precious water to combat overheating is repeated wetting for evaporative cooling—of the back of the neck and the forehead.

It is important in cold country to be aware of conditions that sabotage heat production. Such stresses as fatigue, wet skin, altitude, poor health, hunger, anxiety and lack of adequate prior conditioning will all make it harder to get warm once chilling occurs. So if the body is under stress or conditions are extreme, take extra precautions against chilling and pay attention to the body's warning system.

So what's the best strategy for staying comfortable and warm, but not wet? Breathability adherents claim water vapor will be satisfactorily dispersed if you put porous fabrics next to the body and avoid sealed (waterproof) fabrics. Unfortunately breathability doesn't work, except under ideal conditions when it's not needed. Porous fabrics simply don't pass enough water vapor, and evaporative heat loss is ignored.

In stark contrast to breathability, the vapor barrier approach takes clever advantage of body function .Instead of unrealistically trying to rid the body of moisture while ignoring accompanying heat loss, vapor barriers contain body moisture and reduce its production while stopping heat loss. In short, breathability tries in vain to keep you dry. Vapor barriers aim to keep you warm and comfortably moist while your clothes and insulation stay dry.

A vapor barrier is simply a sealed or waterproof fabric *worn close to the skin* to keep body moisture in instead of trying to drive it out. Don't groan with vision of steamy streaming skin. That needn't happen. Though sealed garments worn *away* from the body over clothing (like waterproof parkas) *can* cause oceans of condensation, sealed fabric worn *close* to the skin produces a startlingly different effect. Body heat makes the

Cold feet? put them in baggies ...and put on a hat!

difference. Because it protects that moist layer of water vapor covering the skin, optimum humidity is easily maintained with minimal vapor output. Given ideal conditions of moisture and heat, the body gratefully closes sweat glands and shuts down vapor production up to 85%.

Vapor Barrier Magic

It's ironic that striving for dry skin only makes it pump more moisture, while permitting skin humidity shrinks production of perspiration! Not only does the wearer escape the steam room condensation associated with sealed garments, clothing worn over the vapor barrier stays completely dry. The severe heat loss that always accompanies sweating is prevented, and the body's water needs (thirst) are proportionally reduced. With the efficient retention of body heat, the outdoor traveler enjoys remarkable warmth with far less of the heavy, bulky, expensive insulation we've come to think is vital in cold weather. In fact the colder it is, the better vapor barriers perform. And there isn't the slightest reduction in efficiency when conditions turn wet and humid. It isn't until the weather grows warm that vapor barriers begin to lose their value, and that's simply because they're so effective at retaining heat.

If you didn't bring vapor barrier clothing with you, you may still be able to enjoy their benefits if you happen to have plastic bags, Saran Wrap, sizeable garbage or trash bags or waterproof parka shell or pants, or plastic clothes or rain suits. If you suffer from cold feet, you can discover the benefits of vapor barriers easily. Slip a plastic bag over your bare foot (or wrap it in Saran Wrap), fold the top around your ankle and put on your normal socks and boots. Not only will your foot stay dramatically warmer, at the end of the day, instead of the bagful of sweat you probably expect, there will be nothing more than faint dampness, and your sock will be totally clean and dry. To prove to yourself how well VB socks work, try it on just one foot, and compare.

Make Yourself a VB Vest

A big trash or garbage bag makes an admirable covering for your torso once you cut holes for your arms and head to make yourself a plastic vest. Put it on next to the skin (preferably), tuck it in your pants, then put on a relatively snug shirt or sweater that will hold the vest close against your body. Put on a light jacket if you want, but don't bundle up. A waterproof rain shell or wind shirt makes an excellent VB shirt ir you wear it next to the skin and cover it with a sweater. So does a rain suit or any waterproof (vapor barrier) garment or covering. And on your next trip in cold country, resolve to gring, in addition to bags for your feet and a VB shirt or vest, a handful of cheap thin (painter's) polyethelene gloves to keep your hands substantially warmer under mittens or gloves.

Think of a VB shirt as a magic undershirt that lets you leave your big heavy jacket at home. It will double as a windbreaker

Make a "magic" VB undershirt by snipping holes in a big trash bag and wearing it next to the skin ...tucked in.

TRASH KING

outer shirt

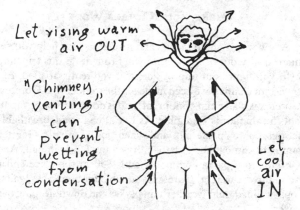

Let rising warm air OUT

"Chimney" venting" can prevent wetting from condensation

Let cool air IN

and even triple as raingear, and I know of no more valuable emergency or survival garment. Properly used, VB clothing will increase your body warmth by an astounding 20°F. The colder it is, the better they work, and they're cheap, light and low on bulk.

If you can't manufacture vapor barrier warmth from what you brought along, or if it isn't cold enough to try, your best bet for obtaining moderate warmth is to wear (ideally) thin layers of loose-fitting dry clothing and rely more on ventilation than breathability to minimize condensation. The easiest way to get rid of warm air and excess humidity is to help it flow out apertures in garments (like an open neck). Take advantage of the fact that heat rises. If air is permitted to flow vertically through a garment, cool air will enter at the bottom and warm air will escape at the top. That's what carries smoke up a chimney so it's called the "chimney effect." Simply put on a pullover shirt or sweater that fastens tightly around the throat and tuck it into your pants. Then exercise until excess body heat is generated. Now untuck your shirt and open the collar and note how much cooler you rapidly become. You can feel the cool air entering at the waist and the warm air flowing up around your throat.

Make Your Clothes Work

A few words about fabrics and insulators may help you get more utility out of the clothes you brought on this trip, and help you figure out improvements if you're dissatisfied. Extravagant claims have been made for the wonder film Goretex. Goretex is water and windproof, and it does pass water vapor, but the amount is negligible. As I've already said, breathable fabrics don't do the job, and when you glue on a Goretex laminate you cut the breathability of any fabric in half. And Goretex in a parka commonly adds $50 to the price and a pound to the weight. Goretex is suitable for bivy sacks, gaiter tops, unlined mild weather rain parkas and down sleeping bag covers.

Using a rough rule of thumb, at 20°F it takes a quarter inch of insulation to keep a backpacker warm while he's walking. Sitting around camp it takes an inch, and when he's sleeping it takes 2-3 inches. Down has always been the premier insulator for backpackers, but don't let that billowy jacket fool you. Under the outer shell are sewn through seams that compress insulation to zero, crisscrossing you with a grid of cold spots, and down's vulnerability to wetting is positively dangerous if you bet your life on it in the snow. Wet down is totally useless, weighs a ton and cannot be dried in the field. Down clothing worn day after day, grows heavier and less effective as it absorbs body moisture—unless you wear a vapor barrier under it.

Polyester batting (Polarguard, Kodasoft, Hollofil, etc.) has different drawbacks. It's heavier than down, doesn't loft as well, and is comparatively short lived. The fibers gradually interlock or align with the friction of use aggravated by compression and heat. Matting occurs, resilience disappears and the loft that yielded insulation is permanently lost. Infrequently used parkas kept cool and never compressed may appear to last for years. Heavily used or abused garments can "go flat" (lose half their loft) in six months.

Pile has become very popular because its insulation is uniform and it doesn't die like polyester or soak up water like down. But it's heavy, bulky, and the wind blows right through. It isn't meant to be used as an outer garment, except in mild weather. Ideally, pile sweaters should have underarm zippers for ventilation. I never wear wool pullover sweaters because they're hard to take on and off and provide no ventilation control. But wool's greatest drawback is that it sponges up sweat or rain readily and is cold and heavy to wear when saturated and very slow to dry.

A Clothing Critique

Vests, because they are open at the armpit, permit ventilation while keeping the trunk warm...If you haven't tried polypropylene underwear for cold weather, you're missing out. This single layer totally non-absorbent weave doesn't itch or cling, is featherwright, cheap, stretchy, comfortable and remarkably warm...A majority of backpackers probably still wear jeans, even though they are uncomfortably tight, heavy, hot and water absorbent. When I wore them

wax
rubbed on
where
the rain hits
Keeps
legs dry
without
sweating.

felt hats
become cooler
after a little
judicious snipping.

regularly, I used to waterproof the surfaces most exposed to
rain (top of the thigh and back of the calf) by rubbing them
with the cake of wax from my fly-tying tying kit... In
Switzerland I learned that you can hike all day on snow or ice
in shorts without chilling your legs—as long as you are careful
to keep your torso well warmed.

Veteran outdoor travelers know the value of headgear, even
if, like me, they don't particularly like hats. When it's cold or
windy, head coverings are vital for the simple reason that since
capillaries in the head and neck don't contract when chilled,
heat loss can be enormous. Protecting the head's warmth can
make the difference between overall comfort and dangerous
chilling. Remember the old axiom: if your feet get cold, put on
a hat. The back of some hat brims need to be turned up,
perhaps fastened with a safety pin, to avoid constant rubbing
when a pack is worn. Felt hats become cooler and lighter when
scissors are used judiciously to cut holes for ventilation.

Bandana handkerchiefs are so endlessly useful that I
sometimes take two. Extremes of temperature, wind and cold,
cause noses to run, and Kleenex is extremely impractical on
the trail. Besides their usefulness as handkerchiefs, bandanas
often serve as hot pads, dish towels, neckerchiefs for protec-

tion against sunburn and insects, compresses, hand towels, large bandages, napkins, slings, wash cloths, etc.

If you'd like to know more about the body's reactions, vapor barriers, clothing selection, the properties of fabrics, coatings and insulation, see my *Pleasure Packing for the '80's*.

Boots

Your boots, of course, should have been thoroughly inspected and tested before you set forth to be sure they were in good shape and fit well. You should have used silicone or Snoseal on vegetable tanned leather and Neatsfoot oil on oil-tanned leather if waterproofing was needed. When it isn't, avoid it in the interests of better breathability and less sweaty feet. If you must seal boot seams in the field, try Chapstick, Crisco, bacon grease, salad oil, etc. Since the backpacker revolt against big heavy leather boots, more and more hikers find themselves delighted with the new lightweight non-leather boots and even sturdy running shoes. We worried at first about destroying our feet, but when it didn't happen we found we could hike miles further with less overheating and no blisters—in fact, no break-in.

And it doesn't really matter if they get wet splashing through a creek because they dry quickly and the water does no damage. You likewise needn't worry that a high top is needed for ankle support. The vast majority of sprains, twists and related injuries occur well below the ankle bone. Even the most rigid high top boots do not always protect against such injuries. And keep an open mind on sole tread. The lug soles most people insist on are good on forest paths and gravel, but aren't so good in mud because they clog quickly, and they're inferior on some slick surfaces like bare rock... Bailing wire scrounged from old campsites can be used to replace rotten cotton or leather laces if you haven't any nylon line or cord.

Socks

Whatever your footgear, I hope you brought along good socks to match, not old or worn out pairs or cheap cotton work socks that stretch horribly. There is no single best sock or sock combination. Too much depends on the fit of the boot, the temperatures expected, the terrain, the tendency of the feet to sweat, skin sensitivity, etc. But it is generally true that too many pairs (too thick a layer) of socks reduces boot support and increases friction, and too thin a layer can be just as bad. The choice is generally between a single heavy sock by itself and the same sock worn over a light inner sock. Generally, less sock is needed on easy terrain in well broken-in boots. Two heavy pairs of socks may be advisable for stiff boots or cross-country hiking likely to be hard on the feet.

Whereas moisture absorption is to be avoided in most garments, in warmer weather it is the aim in socks to sponge up sweat and hold it as far from the skin as possible. Since wool is unexcelled in absorbing and holding moisture without matting or losing resiliency, it is the preferred material for socks, even though damp wool socks are slow to dry. Synthetic fabrics absorb no moisture, and cotton, though highly absorbent, collapses into a hopeless, shapeless soggy mess when wet. Avoid it like the plague and half your socks problems are already solved.

I hope it doesn't sound contradictory to say dry socks are vital to happy feet. Wet, clean socks are far harder on feet than dirty, dry ones. Experienced hikers tend to do far more sock washing and sock changing than beginners, and they take off their boots and air (or wash) their feet at every opportunity. People unaccustomed to walking are likely to suffer from tender feet. Foot powders, Benzoin skin toughener and alcohol rubs may help, but are no substitute for adequate conditioning.

A good case can be made for carrying camp boots on the basis of sensible foot care. Many people like old tennis shoes, but feet tend to sweat in canvas and rubber shoes. I prefer Zoris (also known as thongs and go-aheads) because they are extremely light and air the feet, though they offer scant protection. I have developed the habit, once the day's hiking is done, of immediately taking off my boots (before the sweat dries), washing and rubbing my feet, washing my socks and hanging them in a tree, then slipping on Zoris—if temperature and terrain permit. Sometimes I day hike in sturdy sandals.

Foot Care Tips

A backpacking doctor says, "At the first hint of discomfort, stop, take off the boot and have a look. Wash and dry a place that is getting red, then tape a thin sheet of foam rubber over the spot." I had always relied on moleskin for covering blisters and inflamed places on my feet. Moleskin's disadvantage is that once it is stuck directly to the injured or tender area it cannot safely be removed (without removing the skin) until the end of the trip. In the meantime, of course, the moleskin is certain to get damp and dirty, encouraging bacteria growth. On his advice I have switched to either Molefoam or foam rubber and find both perfectly satisfactory. If I run out, I can steal a fragment from a corner of my mattress.

Often as important as bandaging an inflamed foot, is attacking the cause of the inflamation. On occasion I have had to hammer down a nail with a piece of granite or whittle away a protruding ridge of leather. More often the problem is solved by kneading new boots that pinch, removing a pebble, loosening laces, removing the wrinkle from a sock, adding an extra pair of socks, or changing to a dry pair.

Long toenails will make boots seem too short and can be painfully crippling on downhill stretches. Cutting long toenails the night before a trip will result in pain and inflammation on the trail. Great discomfort (and holes in your socks) can be prevented by awareness of the problem.

Solo Travel Precautions

From a safety standpoint, the greatest danger in wild country is traveling alone. Unfortunately, some of the joys of wilderness travel are only to be discovered by traveling alone. I mostly hike by myself but, recognizing the danger, I try to minimize it by taking all possible precautions. I urge you to do likewise.

I tell someone responsible where I am going, what route I plan to follow both directions, when I expect to be back and the latest time (the time to begin worrying) that I could possibly be back. If the trip will take several days, I usually draw the route on an old map and make an "X" where I expect to spend the nights. Lastly, I indicate in a general way my preparation for emergencies (tent, first aid kit, extra food and clothes), so the urgency of my situation can be judged if I fail to return.

I fervently hope that you brought along a first aid kit appropriate to the trip and a booklet on the treatment of common difficulties. If not, resolve to do so on your next trip. Don't wait until a party member is injured and you're helpless to aid him. See my *Pleasure Packing* for a discussion of first aid kits and how to build your own. You'll also learn that soap and plenty of water are better than antiseptics and first aid creams, and that tourniquets are dangerous and rarely essential since pressure and elevation should stop all but the most serious bleeding. Amateurs should never attempt to set broken bones, but splinting and immobilizing breaks is part of first aid. Seriously injured patients can be taken out to a doctor if they can travel; otherwise bring the doctor in. The following should enable you to treat the most common maladies.

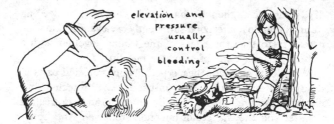

elevation and
pressure
usually
control
bleeding.

Treating Shock & Bleeding

Shock is a state produced by injury or fright. The victim feels cold and clammy and weak. The treatment is to lay the patient down on level ground and make him as comfortable as possible, usually by loosening constricting clothing and covering him if it is cold, until a feeling of well-being returns.

In case of a small or slightly bleeding wound, bleeding usually will soon stop if the wound is elevated so it lies higher than the heart and pressure is applied with a gauze pad. (For a cut foot or leg, the patient lies down and props his leg against a tree; a cut hand should be held above the head.) A large or heavily bleeding wound may have to be closed by hand pressure. A puncture can be firmly blocked by the palm or a finger. On a slice or cut it may be necessary to draw the edges together with the fingers before applying pressure. Closing the wound to stop the bleeding is vital. Once bleeding has been controlled, the wound should be kept elevated to reduce the blood flow and aid clotting. Never attempt to substitute a tourniquet for these procedures.

As soon as bleeding is under control, the wound should be washed with soap and water, or irrigated with water, to carry away bacteria and dirt. It may be necessary during the washing to keep the wound elevated to lessen bleeding. Once cleaned, it may be gently blotted dry with a clean cloth or towel (not to mention toilet paper or clean socks). The clean, dry wound can then be bandaged. On heavily bleeding wounds that do not respond sufficiently to elevation, it may be necessary to tape the edges of the wound together with a butterfly bandage in order to stop bleeding.

Minor cuts and scratches, especially on protected parts of the body, are better left un-bandaged. Protected but uncovered wounds are more easily kept clean and dry; healing is faster and the chances of infection are lower. Antiseptics (mercurichrome, iodine, methiolate and the like) should not be applied; they tend to do more harm than good—inhibiting scab formation and trapping bacteria which cause infection. Small wounds need only bandaids. Larger ones will require a gauze pad held in place by narrow strips of adhesive tape. The largest may require wrapping the limb or body with roll gauze. Gauze and adhesive bandages should be applied directly on top of a wound held closed by a butterfly bandage.

The greatest enemy of wounds is dampness. A wet bandage inhibits healing by providing a favorable environment for the growth of bacteria. Once a bandage has become wet, whether from blood, perspiration or water, it is a menace to health and should be replaced. No bandage at all is far superior to a wet one. The drier the wound the less the chance of infection.

Dealing with Sprains

Nothing is more common among backpackers accustomed to doing their walking on sidewalks than turned or sprained

sprained ankles can be chilled in icy streams or with snow-filled plastic bags

ankles. Severity varies greatly. Some sprains amount to nothing more than a momentary twinge. Others require the victim to be immobilized immediately. Often the wisest course for the person who has suffered a bad sprain (the ankle immediately turning black and blue) is to apply a tape cast and head for the car before the ankle can swell and stiffen.

Moderate sprains should immediately be treated with cold to constrict blood flow and prevent swelling. Putting the foot in an icy rill or applying cold compresses made by filling plastic bags with snow or ice water are fast and effective. Elevating the ankle also helps greatly to reduce the swelling. If sources of cold are not handy or it is inconvenient to stop, an elasticized ankle brace of three-inch Ace bandage may be applied.

Braces are likely to be carried only by people with weak ankles who have come to rely on them. Ace bandages have the advantage of being usable on other parts of the body. In either case, it may be necessary to remove all (or at least the outer) socks to make room for the bandage in the boots. And people (like myself) who have sensitive Achilles tendons may find it impossible to wear an elastic bandage very long. Bandages need only be worn while walking. They should be removed at night and at any other time that the ankle can be elevated.

All of the swelling that is going to take place will happen on the day of the sprain or the day that follows. On the third day, with the swelling stopped, the treatment changes from the application of cold to the application of heat. The intent now is to stimulate blood flow through the injured area in order to reduce swelling. Hot compresses made from bandanas, towels, diapers, or washrags dipped in heated water are excellent, or the ankle can be baked before an open fire. Hot water bottles can sometimes be fashioned from large plastic bags, but care must be taken not to burn the patient. The exception to heat treatment is the ankle which is immediately encased in a cast of tape. Such casts should be left undisturbed for two or three days and heat applied only after removal.

Snakebite

While rattlesnake bites are uncommon, a snakebite kit ought to be carried in snake country. First prerequisites in prevention are caution and the ability to recognize poisonous snakes and the sort of terrain they like. I have spent a good deal of time in heavily infested areas and have encountered a great many rattlers. But by never extending any part of my body into a concealed place that could contain a snake, I have avoided being bitten. Although the Cutters kit offers more elaborate and valuable instruction, the treatment can be summarized in three words: "Cut, Suck, Tie" (the order is important). Avoid the tendency to cut too deep (¼ inch is sufficient) and tie too tight (let the tourniquet just dent the skin). Since suction cups are useless on any but flat, fleshy, hairless skin, mouth suction will often be required. Once first aid is given the patient should be made to rest to restrict blood circulation. He should also be taken to a hospital.

Salt pills (5 grain) are not required by most people unless the perspiration is literally pouring off the body. The usual dosage in such cases is one pill every 4-8 hours, but only while drinking a quart of water per 1-2 pills. Overdosing on salt is dangerous! Poison oak, like rattlesnakes, is a hazard that can usually be avoided by caution and the ability to recognize the danger. Poison oak in the west (and poison ivy in the east) have oily-looking distinctive three-lobed leaves that are easily remembered once they have been identified. Tolerance to the oil, which remains potent for some time on clothes and on the fur of pets, varies widely. Persons exposed have a second chance to avoid the itching, easily-spread rash, by scrubbing exposed skin vigorously with soap and hot water on the same day. Skin irritation generally begins four to five hours after exposure. In the west, poison oak rarely grows above 6000 feet.

Sunburn vs. Tan

Sunburn is a constant threat, especially at higher altitudes, to city dwellers who are not deeply tanned. At 6000 feet the skin burns twice as fast as at sea level, and the liability continues to increase with altitude. Sunburn often ruins a trip when a pale backpacker tries for a fast tan. Precautions should be taken to cover—or at least shade—all parts of the body for most of the day. Few people ever acquire a deep enough tan to expose themselves all day at high altitude without burning. Special care should be taken to avoid burning the nose to prevent starting a cycle of peeling, burning and repeeling.

Nothing is worse than having to hike in the heat completely shrouded from the sun—unless it is suffering with sunburned shoulders that will have to carry a pack the next day. Trying to safely tan white skin by short periods of exposure to fierce high altitude sun is a bothersome, inconvenient process on a backpacking trip. Potent sun screen ointment is essential on most trips. So is protection for the lips. The best treatment for sunburned skin is to keep it clean and dry, but I prefer, after washing gently in the evening, to lightly rub in petroleum jelly, wiping off the excess. For the inevitable burns from fire or stove, I also rely on petroleum jelly rather than carry a burn ointment.

Beware Sunglasses

It isn't widely known that sunglasses often do more harm than good. They trick the eyes into staying open wider than they should in bright conditions, resulting in eyestrain. And the darkened lenses block out healthful rays which are essential to the body. A wide-brimmed hat or sunshade is always preferable. "Dark glasses are a crutch," said the old prospector with whom I used to travel on the desert. "Put them on when it's bright and you'll never take them off." He taught me to squint and wear my hat low for a couple of days to acclimate my eyes, rather than develop a dependency on shades. And it works. I only wear sunglasses now under extreme conditions.

Murl also taught me to use "Indian sunglasses" when vision was vital under extra bright conditions. Put the tips of your middle fingers together, end to end, then tuck the tips of your index fingers together tight against them, just beneath. Hold your four fingertips against your nose in the hollow beneath your brow and look through the easily adjustable slits between your fingers. Now your shaded eyes can stop squinting and open wide for maximum vision, even when looking almost into the sun.

If you need bug repellant in quantity it makes sense to buy the diethyl metatoluamide at the drugstore and make your own dilution. A dosage of 200 milligrams/day of vitamin B-1 taken orally will make your perspiration repellent to mosquitos and thus keep them away. So will the heavy consumption of garlic.

Altitude Sickness

As altitude increases the oxygen content of the air decreases. In order to adjust, the body strives to process more air by means of faster and deeper breaths, to better extract oxygen from the air. Adjustment begins at only slight elevation, but shortness of breath and dizziness do not usually appear until about 7000 feet. Individual tolerance to altitude varies widely. The more gradual the change in altitude, the easier the acclimatization. The well-rested, vigorous, healthy individual usually acclimatizes easily. Smoking, drinking and heavy eating before or during a climb make acclimatization difficult.

Failure of the body to adjust to reduced oxygen intake results in "altitude" or mountain sickness. Mild symptoms include headache, lassitude, shortness of breath and a vague feeling of illness—all of which usually disappear after a day of rest. Acute mountain sickness is marked by severe headache, nausea, vomiting, insomnia, irritability and muddled thinking. The victim must descend to a lower elevation. Mountain sickness can usually be avoided by beginning a trip in good condition, spending a night at the trailhead before starting out and choosing modest goals for the first day's walk. Most acclimatization occurs in the first two or three days.

People who acclimatize poorly, when they reach elevations in excess of 10,000 feet, are susceptible to high altitude pulmonary edema (HAPE) (fluid accumulation in the lungs). The first symptons include a dry, persistent, irritating cough, anxiety, and an ache beneath the breast bone and shortness of breath. If the victim is not evacuated promptly to lower elevation or given oxygen, breathing may become rapid, noisy and difficult, the skin often takes on a bluish tinge, and death may occur quickly.

Hypothermia

The number one killer of outdoor travelers is Hypothermia, defined as "rapid mental and physical collapse due to chilling of the body's core." When the body loses heat faster than it's being produced, you instinctively exercise to keep warm while the body cuts back blood supply to the extremities. Both drain your energy reserves. If chilling and exposure continue, cold will reach the brain, depriving you of judgment and reasoning power without your awareness. As chilling progresses, you lose control of your hands and body When your body can no longer summon reserves to prevent the drop in core temperature, stupor, collapse and death await.

The first line of defense is awareness, awareness that most hypothermia cases occur during mild temperatures, 30-50°F. The greater hazards are wind and wet. Wind drives away the skin's cushion of warm air, and it refrigerates wet clothing.

Remember that 50°F water is unbearably cold, and that the wet body can lose heat 200 times as fast as one protected by dry clothing! There is no better clothing for hypothermia protection than vapor barriers. If you can't stay dry and warm, do whatever is necessary to stop exposure. Turn back, give up, get out, make camp—before exhaustion can complicate your plight. Don't shrug off shivering. If you have to exercise continuously to prevent it, you're in danger. Get out of wet clothes, get dry and put on vapor barriers to stop heat loss, then take hot drinks, heap on the insulation, utilize whatever heat sources are available and stay awake.

By paying attention to what your body tells you, by proper use of your clothes, and by taking precautions against injury, you can double your chances of enjoying a safe, happy trip.

THREE
Camping

Since the average backpacker spends at least half his time in camp, a happy trip depends on his ability to consistently pick the best possible spot to camp, and then to develop it for maximum shelter, safety and comfort. Some of my camping routines may be helpful.

A persistent wind, damp ground, sloping bedsites, a lack of fuel or shelter, noisy neighbors, clouds of mosquitos, lack of water, etc., will rob the best equipped party of a pleasant night. There are times, of course, when bad weather, poor planning, inhospitable country or just plain bad luck make a terrible location unavoidable. The veteran backpacker will choose the least terrible site and devise the most ingenious development in order to make it yield minimal comfort.

First priority in site selection must go to bedsites since nothing is more important than a good night's sleep. Damp and sloping ground should be avoided—so should roots and rocks that cannot be removed. Spare clothing and equipment should not be forgotten in the struggle to make a poor bedsite passable. Shelter from wind, unwelcome sun, evening downdrafts or intense cold may be essential to restful sleep.

As many a beginning camper has learned the hard way, there's more to a good bed than sleeping bag, mattress and ground cloth. A well-chosen, well-prepared bedsite may be even more important. Practiced backpackers will recognize a good place. Beginners will need to consider various criteria. The chief enemies of a good night's sleep are cold, dampness, wind, insects, running water, flying sparks, falling widow-makers, avalanche and the snoring of one's companion.

The most common mistake is to select a depression, dry ravine, streambank or dried up snowpool because it is sheltered from the afternoon wind. But winds have a habit of disappearing around dusk, turning an unfriendly promontory into an admirable camp. As the evening advances, a gentle but persistent night wind commonly rises to pour cold heavy air down the streambeds and ravines and into those inviting depressions, leaving them as much as ten degrees colder than higher ground only a few feet away.

Dry ravines and snow pools, besides collecting cold air at night, also collect running water quickly in a cloudburst.

hollows can turn into puddles.

Meadows tend to be damp and attract heavy dew. Dew results when moist air cools, causing a fallout of condensation. Dew will be heavier near a lake, stream or meadow, and just after a storm. Heavy dew is capable of severely wetting an unprotected sleeping bag in just a few hours. Woe to the weary backpacker who, late on a night of heavy dew, has to climb inside a drenched bag left open or inside out.

Choosing a Bedsite

There are enough advantages to sleeping beneath a tree to more than compensate for the filtered view of the stars. Trees serve as an umbrella to shield the sleeper from heavy dew and light rain. On a bitterly cold, clear night sheltering branches serve as insulation from solar radiation. The air temperature beneath a tree may be ten degrees warmer than a bedsite exposed to the chill night sky. Since I rarely want to be awakened at dawn, I regularly position my bed to the west of a good sized tree so that it can shade me from the early morning sun. The shade allows me to sleep an hour or so past sunrise without being cooked in my mummy bag. Trees frequently serve as windbreaks, clothes hangers, pack supports, tarp tie-downs, and a source of cushioning pine-needle mattresses. (The cutting of living boughs for a mattress can no longer be justified.)

It is generally important to know the direction of the prevailing wind in camp and to use this information in locating a bedsite, especially if the weather is unsettled or threatening. Even on a still night it is a bad idea to sleep directly downwind of the campfire. A wind in the night can fan the coals and bombard the bed with glowing sparks, each of which will burn a neat round hole in the nylon fabric. If the fire is utterly dead the sleeper will instead receive a shower of ashes. Badly placed beds are rarely forgotten.

Bedsites need to be very nearly level. If there must be a

slope, it should run downhill from head to feet. Sleeping on a sidehill is nothing short of torture. One is generally better off with an inferior level site than a sloping bed that is otherwise perfect. It is not uncommon for the sleeper who made his bed on a slope to wake up in the morning ten feet away with the distinct impression of not having slept at all. I believe strongly that a bedsite's most important characteristic is its susceptibility to alteration, and I have yet to encounter one I could not improve.

As I view potential sites, bare earth is fine, deep pine-needles or duff are perfect, decayed tree trunks are excellent—when not inhabited by ants—sand and gravel are satisfactory, provided I am carrying a cushioning foam mattress. Grass is poor because it cannot be contoured without removing the roots and permanently scaring the ground.

When I have selected the best available bedsite in all respects and decided where my head is to be, I dig a rectangular hip and shoulder hole. It measures about 18 inches wide, 28 inches long and 2½ inches deep with sloping sides and a slightly concave bottom. All of the excavated earth or sand is heaped into a pillow about three inches thick. From the bottom of the hip hole to the bottom of the foot area, I smooth the ground, removing sticks, rocks, pine-cones and twigs. If the ground is sloping, I often use the earth excavated from the hip hole to build up the area that supports the legs, finding some other way to make a pillow. For maximum comfort, the feet should be a little higher than the hips and I find it well worth the trouble to make sure that they are. In

an earth pillow and a shoulder-hip hole contour the ground to fit the body.

seriously sloping or less than level ground it is sometimes easier to dig the hip hole deeper rather than pad the leg area.

Bed Building

Once the preliminary shaping is complete, I lie down on the bedsite on my back to test the contours. If the shoulder section needs widening and the hip hole deepening, I scratch some kind of a pattern with a twig, then get up to make alterations. When I lie down a second time, if everything feels comfortable (nothing pressing or cramped) I roll over on my side. This will generally feel less comfortable and additional excavating will be needed at the point of the hip and thigh. But I dig with restraint, knowing that no hole can fit perfectly both ways. The results must be a compromise which favors the position in which one usually sleeps.

In an attempt to make a perfectly contoured hip hole, the novice will often build up an area to support the small of the back. This is a grave mistake and is guaranteed to produce an aching back before dawn. Women, because of their broader hips, usually are less comfortable on the ground than men; they will want a deeper hiphole that tapers to a shallower shoulder hole.

My contouring operation may seem a waste of time to some, but I can think of no better investment of time than the five minutes it takes me to transform a small strip of earth into a comfortable bed that will insure me eight hours of restful sleep.

If the wind is blowing and cannot be avoided I take pains to point my feet to windward, and if the night promises to be cold I build a small earth and rock windbreak at my feet. Even on a warm night a persistent wind can chill exposed limbs; the noise, the twitching of the bag and the breeze in one's face will rob even—perhaps especially—the most exhausted

this snug sleeper is shaded from the early morning sun and sheltered from the chilly night sky.

camper of hours of sleep. On an evening when the wind promises to blow, an extra fifteen minutes spent hunting for or constructing shelter from the wind will be time well spent.

After making my bed under the stars, I take pains to protect it from dew. Many campers don't realize that moisture condensing from body and breath inside a sleeping bag can weigh 2-3 pounds. If you don't or can't dry your bed in the morning

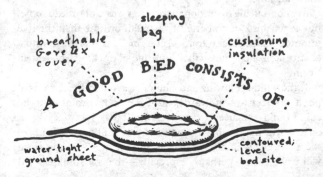

A GOOD BED CONSISTS OF:

breathable Gore tex cover

sleeping bag

cushioning insulation

water-tight ground sheet

contoured, level bed site

before you pack up, you'll not only carry that moisture, your bag will lose a significant portion of its loft (warmth) as a result. The heat lost along with that 2-3 pounds of body moisture, it has been calculated, would be sufficient to melt 27 pounds of ice! Much of that wasted energy can be saved, and your bag made an impressive 20°F warmer, by using a vapor barrier liner or sleeping in VB clothing. Consider that for your next trip if you're cold on this one. It's a lot cheaper and lighter than buying a warmer bag.

Vapor Barriers in Bed

A cruder but still effective way to increase your bag's warmth is to wear your clothing to bed. Ideally, wear it over VB clothing so you stay warmer and don't sweat it up. But you don't need to carry a 20°F bag just because the temperature might get that low. You can carry a lighter, cheaper 30°F bag and rely on the clothing you have to carry anyway to provide the other 10°F capability. Don't wear down clothes to bed without a VB shirt underneath unless you want them to get wet. You can also increase the warmth of your bag by wearing a watchcap, or balaclava, or otherwise covering your head and face to prevent heat loss than can chill the entire body. Or, before your next trip, make yourself a 6-12" diameter "breathing plug" out of inch-thick open-celled sheet foam to seal the opening in your hood without inhibiting your breathing in the slightest.

For camping warmly and comfortably on snow, you can cheaply and easily build a better, safer bed of plastic and foam than the finest down bag made. You'll find plans for making it and its companion the "Wood Hood" in my *Pleasure Packing for the '80's.*

Sleeping in a mummy bag on the ground in the wilderness is not much like sleeping in a heated home, but too many people, it seems to me, blame the resultant strangeness and likely wakefulness on the shape or confining nature of the bag. The hooded mummy bag is so much more satisfactory in the long run than its larger hoodless relatives that an effort should be made to accept its confines. Except in dry warm climates, down beds should be protected on the outside by tents, bivy sacks or Goretex, and on the inside by vapor barriers for maximum safety and efficiency.

Most of us must find some way to elevate and cushion our heads if we wish to sleep in any kind of comfort. Half the problem is solved during site preparation by making an earth pillow. Cushioning is generally supplied by a down parka stuffed into one of its own sleeves or the sleeping bag stuff bag filled with spare clothing.

With a comfortable rest carefully prepared for, I sort through my pack and dig out everything I am liable to need in the night: personal kit, watch cap, bandana, flashlight, down sweater and socks for the following day. All of these are tucked in appropriate spots beside my sleeping bag inside the bivouac cover; a rock on top of my pillow assures that nothing will be dampened by the dew that will fall before I finally go to bed. In the process of digging through my pack, I collect everything needed for preparing dinner: packets of soup and stew, herbs, condiments, pots, cups, stove, etc.

Sheltering the Stove

Since even a small breeze disturbs the flame and reduces the efficiency of most stoves, it's advisable to locate the kitchen in the most sheltered, protected part of camp. The alternative, especially if preparation requires a low flame, is to build a wind screen of some sort.

If the stove won't light in the most sheltered spot available, I pull the six-foot foam pad from my bed, bend it into a circle around the stove and try again.

Once the stove is set up, water drawn from the lake, and the

oatmeal, coming up!

soup packet emptied in the pot, I know I am no more than fifteen minutes away from enjoying the first course of dinner. If hunger and approaching darkness do not urge me to start cooking, I usually see what can be done about preparing a campfire to cheer up the evening.

If my campsite has been used before, I use or rebuild the existing firepit, taking care to turn the blackened sides of the rocks inward so I do not add to their discoloring. If I am on virgin ground, I try to dig a shallow pit in sand or mineralized earth (never duff, meadow, decayed wood or vegetation) so that I can safely build a fire without blackening anything.

If firewood isn't plentiful, I make my small campfire using rotten wood which another winter will render unburnable, chunks of bark, smashed pine cones and other junk wood. Since chunks of charcoal are unsightly in the wilderness, I try to burn all that I find in a campsite, as well as all the fuel I use, down to an ash which will blow away and convert quickly to soil.

At sunset or thereabouts, I light the stove beneath my soup, put on warm clothes for the evening, zip extra food securely into my pack, stir the soup to make sure it is not sticking, adding whatever butter, milk or bacon bar I can spare. If it's going to be dark before dinner is ready, I light and nurse my campfire past the critical stage. The best single rule I know for successful firebuilding is for the fire builder to be supplied with twice the tinder, matches, twigs, paper, etc., that should be needed.

Firebuilding Tips

A great many fires die while the builder is out looking frantically for more of something that burns well. Other common mistakes are packing the paper too tightly and smothering it with tinder: any kind of fuel needs plenty of oxygen to burn properly. At the other extreme, spreading the fuel so loosely that it fails to concentrate its heat is a familiar cause of failure.

It is generally advisable to schedule dinner so that the meal is over—except for dessert, snacks and drinks—well before dark. I like to go fishing or walking between dinner and dark. These excursions, I have discovered, often turn out to provide the most pleasant experiences of the trip. After a long day, of course, it is easy to lie in camp, feeling comfortably tired, and often I do exactly that.

Since on short trips in small parties I usually do not carry pails, jugs or buckets for carrying water, it is often necessary to refill my plastic bottle. The great advantage of the Mallory flashlight over those requiring conventional sized batteries is that by holding the light in one's mouth both hands are left free for cooking, washing dishes, gathering wood or drawing water. It is even possible, with practice, to carry on a conversation.

When the time approaches to go to bed, I customarily brush my teeth in my last cup of tea and stir up the fire to coax as complete combustion as possible; partially burned sticks make unrewarding scenery. If the night is cold I put on a Navy surplus wool watch cap to ward off the cold (body heat is rapidly lost from the head). If I am putting on pajamas or long johns or other clothes to sleep in I warm them first over the fire and change quickly. I tend the fire until it has burned down to a safe bed of ash and coals. If there is a breeze or danger of traveling sparks, I spread the ashes to reduce heat and cover with sand or water.

There are easier jobs than getting undressed in the cold and dark and wriggling into a dew-soaked mummy bag without getting cold or wet. I generally sit on my pillow, take off my shoes and turn them upside down; then I take off my socks and trousers and slip into bed in a sitting position in my shoulder hole. From this point it is comparatively easy to peel off the rest of my clothes and tuck them under the tarp or bivouac cover before sliding the rest of the way into bed. After pulling the drawstring that converts the top of my bag into a hood, and locking it, I zip up the bag, leaving my flashlight by the top of the zipper.

Drying Out Your Bed

In the morning the first thing I do — after rising and getting on my clothes — is to dismantle my bed and set it to dry. Even if the dew seems already to have dried, there is liable to be ground dampness and condensation from my body. Weather has a way of changing fast in the wilderness, and it is nice to have one's bed bone dry and securely packed; the same goes for tents and tarps; anyone who has had to pack and carry a wet tent will go to some lengths to avoid repeating the experience. I spread my foam pad, bivouac cover and sleeping bag out flat on sunny rocks or breezy bushes until they are warm and absolutely dry, then I turn them over. When the outsides are nicely toasted, I turn them inside out and repeat the process. In the dry air of the high Sierra the whole process rarely takes more than half an hour, even after a heavy dew or drizzle.

Since I am more likely to wake up feeling sticky than hungry I usually wash, or possible swim, before thinking of food. On most summer days my breakfast consists of cold cereal and fruit, along with Sherpa tea, so I am not obliged to clean the stew pot before eating. But if the morning is cold and blustery, and a cold breakfast is unappealing, I clean the pot sufficiently (often by merely wiping it out carefully with a paper towel) to avoid unduly flavoring the hot spicy apple-

relaxing after breakfast

sauce and instant oatmeal I customarily make; if the morning is really foul, I empty in my Birchermuesli too.

After a bad night, a very hard yesterday, or just for fun if there is no great hurry—I like to lie down and take a rest after breakfast on my foam pad. I sometimes read, make notes, study the map and make plans for the day, while lying comfortably on my back. Often I just examine the treetops, and sometimes I accidentally fall asleep.

When it comes time to relieve myself I play a kind of game; I pretend to be a trapper who is traveling in the country of the sharp-eyed, sharp-nosed Sioux, and I hunt for a concealed spot unlikely to be visited by scouting parties—under a deadfall, in a thicket of brush, behind a boulder. I roll away a rock or kick a hole in loose soil, and slip the rubber band from the toilet paper roll around my wrist. When I have made my contribution, I burn the paper, cover the hole and jump on it once or twice to pack down the soil; then I roll back the rock, kick back a covering of leaves, duff or pine needles and branches, artfully landscaping the site until an Indian scout would never give it a second look.

I am careful to avoid any place that might serve as a campsite or trail. Running water, dry streambeds, empty snowmelt pools and any location within a hundred feet of a camp are also shunned. There is anothing more discouraging than finding that the second best campsite in an area has been used as a latrine by the people from the number one camp—unless it is streamers of used toilet paper fluttering in the trees.

Clean Up the Country

In recent years I have increasingly become interested in cleaning up the country. Restoring a quality of wildnesss to the wilds by erasing the blighting marks of man has become one of my chief pleasures in the areas I travel. It seems the least I can do to repay the joy that wilderness has given me—and the one thing I can do to help make it last a little while longer.

It also gives me a sense of accomplishment to restore an ugly site to its previous condition of natural beauty. For instance, a handsome little alpine lake may be marred by a sheet of glittering aluminum foil lying on the bottom. The act of fishing out the foil, crumpling it up and packing it into a corner of the knapsack restores the beauty and naturalness of the setting. Simple acts of this sort, surprisingly enough, can provide immense satisfaction.

I have found that people who endlessly procrastinate about cleaning out their cellars will conscientiously clean up other people's campsites. And children whose rooms at home stand

cleaning
up the
lakeshore
can be
satisfying.

knee deep in litter will patiently pick the broken glass from someone else's fireplace. The fact that "trash begets trash" is as true in the wilds as it is in the city. Let litter accumulate and travelers will feel free to help swell the accumulation. But when a public place has been freshly cleaned people become reluctant to scatter their trash.

Before leaving camp on short excursions—cleanup, fishing, an after dinner stroll—I always take a look around to make sure it is secure against the incursions of small animals, near neighbors, sudden weather change and fire. Brazen chipmunks, mice, bluejays and squirrels have more than once escaped with significant portions of my larder without even waiting for me to walk away from camp. Enticing food should always be stowed in a pack, preferably in a zippered compartment which can be tightly closed, before leaving camp, and the pack should be hung from a tree or rope—depending on the type and voracity of predators.

Camp Security

There was a time when one could leave money lying around camp in perfect safety—provided one was beyond the range of day hikers. Nowadays, it is a good idea not to leave anything valuable in camp. A camp that will be seen by a large number of hikers is far too vulnerable to leave. More than one group of hikers in recent summers has come back from a hike to find their camp entirely vanished. And backpackers in roadhead camps have awakened to find that everything but the bags they were sleeping in was gone. Packs, boots, down bags, parkas and the like have significant resale value and are easily sold, so it pays to protect expensive gear—and to camp well away from the boulevards whenever possible.

It should be a matter of common sense never to leave camp for even a few minutes if a fire is burning. A gust of wind can carry flaming embers into the woodpile, dry pine needles or a two hundred dollar sleeping bag and cause substantial damage in a matter of moments. The fire should be absolutely stone-cold dead whenever camp is left untended. Every summer I pass empty camps in which a fire still burns or smolders. The incidence of man-made fires is climbing every year.

Long excursions from camp require more precautions because weather must also be taken into account. Consider my recent experience. We had left our high Sierra camp close under a mountain on a clear summer day, without any thought of a possible storm. Our mistake was in forgetting that we really had no idea of weather conditions on the other side of the mountain.

By the time we reached the ridge the storm that had been hidden was almost upon us. By the time we returned to camp, late that afternoon, it had been raining steadily for several hours. Fortunately, our clothes and food were safe in our waterproof packs and our sleeping bags, though damp in places, were under tarps. The Bleuet stove was soaked and would not light, but we managed to build a big fire and stood before it in the wind and rain for another long hour before the sun came out a few minutes before sunset. There was just barely time to halfway dry out our beds and get them back under tarps before a drenching dew began to fall. Even

he wasn't ready for rain.

... now he's ruining his boots!

without seeing the sky behind the mountain that morning, I should have been suspicious because the breeze, though faint, was blowing from the south. Wind blowing from the south, east or northeast is liable to bring a storm. Wind from the north, northwest or southwest generally heralds fair weather; the major exceptions are mountain thunderstorms which often come from the west.

Weather Forecasting

Clouds offer the backpacker another aid to weather forecasting. Big fluffy cumulus clouds are harbingers of fair weather—so long as they do not join together and begin to billow upward. When they cease to exist as individual clouds and the bottoms darken and the tops form columns and flattened anvil heads—a thunder storm is on the way. High, thin cirrus clouds are generally filled with ice particles; when they whiten the sky or their mare's tails reach upward, a storm can generally be expected within twenty-four hours.

Stratus clouds, as the name implies, come in waves or layers or bands; when they are smooth and regular and rolling the weather should be fair, but probably cool; when stratus clouds are mottled or fragmented into a buttermilk sky, it will usually storm.

The astute wilderness traveler learns to recognize a number of signs of impending weather change. Sun dogs or halos around the sun forecast rain or snow; so does a ring around the moon. A red sky at dawn or an early morning rainbow, or the absence of dew on the grass—all of these should warn the traveler that bad weather is brewing. So should yellow sunsets and still, ominously quiet moist air.

Sensitivity to the signs should influence the backpacker's choice of camps and trip itinerary. If the signs are bad, he should erect the tent, lay in a good supply of firewood beneath a tarp and schedule close-to-home amusement rather than exposed activities like climbing. On the other hand, a careful reading of the weather may enable him to set out on a climb, confident of good weather, even before the rain has stopped. For instance, clearing can be expected despite heavy clouds, providing "there's enough blue to make a Dutchman a pair of pants."

Storm Warnings

Thunderstorms, those exciting, dramatic, generally short-lived phenomena, are nevertheless frightening to a good many people. I have seen tall trees virtually explode when struck by a bolt of lightning, sending huge limbs flying in every direction. But the danger is negligible for anyone willing to take the necessary precaution—leaving vulnerable locations before the storm begins. The places to avoid are high, open exposed slopes, hills, ridges and peaks, isolated or unusually tall trees, lakes, meadows, or open flats. The safest places are in caves, canyon bottoms and a part of the forest where the trees are comparatively short.

The hiker or climber anxious about lightning usually has considerable warning. When cumulus clouds have darkened and fused and still air has been replaced by sudden erratic winds, the storm is about to break and backpackers should

lightning strikes prominent exposed places.

already be snugly sheltered. Lightning usually appears to be striking closer than it is, especially at night. The distance can be accurately gauged by counting the seconds between flash and boom. Every five seconds in time means a mile in distance. Thirteen seconds between flash and boom means the lightning is striking two and a half miles away. No matter how fierce the storm may seem, summer afternoon thunderstorms characteristically are short, and the chances are good that the sun will be out before sunset. If my camp is battened down and I can watch in some comfort, I enjoy the noisy melodrama of an afternoon storm.

When the time comes to pack up and move camp, I like to see how wild I can make my campsite look. If I have camped on virgin ground, I take pains to restore it to its natural conditions so that a passerby would not guess it had ever been used. There are far too many campsites already in existence; my aim is to decrease, not increase the number. After collecting all the unburned foil and metal from the ashes and packing it in a garbage bag, I bury charcoal, ashes and partially burned twigs or scatter them well back in thick brush.

Demolishing Camp

The firepit is filled in, blackened rocks are hidden and turned black side down in the brush, and the hip and shoulder hold from my bed are filled in and smoothed over. Pine needles, sand, soil, duff, pine cones and branches are scattered naturally about and if the area still faintly resembles a camp I sometimes roll in a few rocks and large limbs or small logs to fill up the bare spots. After firewood is scattered, all that remains are a few footprints. Once rain has fallen it would be difficult to tell that the area ever had been disturbed.

So far we've been talking about camping under benign summer conditions where shelter from a ground cloth, bivy cover or unpitched tarp has been judged sufficient. Now let's

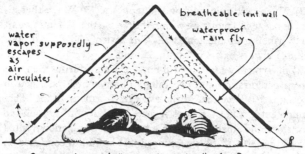

breatheable tent wall

waterproof rain fly

water vapor supposedly escapes as air circulates

Conventional "breatheable?" A-frame

consider a less friendly environment, and therefore let's assume that you brought a tent.

The number one problem in tents—as in clothing—is condensation. Ironically, it's a problem that many have never encountered if their tenting experience is limited to dry, breezy conditions in moderate temperatures. But when condensation strikes, the experience is likely to be intensely unpleasant, even dangerous in extreme conditions.

When water vapor in the tent turns to water on the walls that wets everything it touches and runs down to form puddles on the floor and soaks your sleeping bag, that's extreme condensation. If the temperature is below freezing, the walls turn frosty instead of wet and the frost falls on your bed instead of making puddles under it. Since humans, as we have seen, are constantly producing moisture as they breathe and perspire, the concentration of water vapor in the small volume of a backpacking tent is unavoidably high. If the tent is closed tight against rain, cold or wind, this concentration is likely to increase.

Condensation occurs when the tent wall is colder than the surrounding air—or the air on one side of it. There are three ways this can happen: (1) From cold radiation on still, clear cold nights. (Condensation is rare when the wind is blowing.)

(2) When cold rain falls on the tent, and (3) When there is excess heat and moisture within the tent so that the interior air is warmer than the tent wall. The last of these conditions almost always exists in occupied tents.

You typically lose about 8 cups of water during the night from perspiration and breathing. That vapor is confined in perhaps 70 cubic feet in the average 2-man, A-frame. That much extra water (16 cups if there are 2 of you) is bound to overload the small volume of air unless it's somehow vented from the tent. If it isn't removed it is bound to condense on tent walls whenever they are substantially colder (highly likely) than the air inside.

Tent Condensation Tips

There are a number of things you can do to keep down the moisture level, and they may easily determine whether or not you stay comfortable during conditions ripe for condensation. (1) Be careful not to spill drinking water. (2) If you must cook inside the tent, keep a tight lid on the cook pot and run the stove for a few minutes after dinner to warm up the tent interior so excessive moisture can easily escape from the vent you should have at the peak of the roof. A great many problems and dangers can be avoided by cooking outside. Do so if you possibly can. (3) Use a vapor barrier liner in your sleeping bag and wear vapor barrier clothing to keep you warmer, reduce sweating and dehydration, and avoid sweating up your clothes.

(4) Don't dry those rain or sweat dampened clothes in the tent. If you can't leave sweaty clothes outside, keep them in a closed plastic bag so they don't contribute dampness to the atmosphere. (5) If it's raining or snowing when you enter the tent, take the trouble to shake off excess moisture outside, remove wet outer clothing as you enter and fold it inward on itself to minimize exposure to the air inside. Best of all, use an um-

brella! (6) If the tent leaks rain, try to find the trouble spot. Patch holes with tape and seal leaky seams with sealant right away if possible; otherwise mark leaks for between-trip repairs at home. Leaks generally are small and water often flows unnoticed down walls or seams to form a puddle that may convince you it's the floor that's leaking. Don't be fooled.

(7) Pitch your tent or trench around it so that water cannot run beneath it. The best tub floor should not be mistaken for a boat. Water under a tent is almost certain to enter. (8) Even in dry weather ground dampness has a tendency to rise through waterproof tent floors and condense inside. To protect against this phenomena on damp ground or snow, place an unpunctured polyethelene sheet beneath the tent before you pitch it. (9) Nylon expands when wet, so rain or dew can make your tightly pitched tent sag and flap, which disturbs the insulating air gap between walls and thus cools the inner wall, inviting condensation.

Other Tenting Problems

If you do what you can to reduce moisture and pitch and vent your tent properly, you should rarely encounter significant condensation. But when you do, wipe it off with a small sponge periodically so it won't collect and drip or run down the wall to puddle beneath your bed. If your tent has been a failure, resolve next time to bring one with better chimney venting or higher wall temperatures. A few words about other tent problems may make the choice easier, as well as help you make the tent you brought perform better.

Goretex is poor for tents because its porosity interferes with the chimney venting that actually beats condensation. Tent makers who believe in Gore's claim of a partial-pressure driving force provide no vents to sabatoge it. The results can be horrible condensation where conditions are ripe for it. Cooking in such a tent risks dangerous, even fatal, carbon

tarp tents:

monoxide poisoning. Goretex has proven to produce more frost condensation, whatever the venting, than conventional nylon canopies, coated or uncoated. Finally, as in other applications, Goretex commonly adds to the weight, nearly doubles the cost, is stiff and often noisy.

Treatment of tent fabric with fire-retardent chemicals is now required by law in most states, but don't get careless. Treated tents will still burn. Goretex, incidentally, fails to meet fire retardant standards in five states, including California.

The best way to avoid zipper problems is be gentle, especially where zippers curve and are under tension. Continuous coil zips with soft aluminum sliders often spread until they fail. When that happens, run them back to square one and squeeze the slider back together with pliers to effect a repair. This will work 4-5 times before the zipper must be replaced. The secret in avoiding zipper failure is simply to hold the two edges together before you zip.

Improvising Shelter

Tube tents have declined in popularity as the public discovers that what sounds and looks like a good idea has definite limitations. Because a tube of plastic is completely sealed, it won't leak a drop as long as it's intact, but it may get you and your bed wetter from the oceans of condensation produced than the rain would. Tube tents need both ends wide open to allow sufficient venting to hold down condensation. So for protracted rain they simply aren't practical. But if you brought one you may well find it valuable as backup protection against brief afternoon thundershowers. Temporary shelter from rain may also be rigged out of the tarps you brought along.

For several years I carried a 7 x 9 foot coated fabric poncho. When combined with the 6 x 8 foot plastic ground sheet carried by my partner, it provided us considerable shelter. After carefully preparing the bedsite to reduce the chance of puncture, I used it as a ground sheet, covering my bag on cold or dewy nights. Two corners on one side were fitted with permanent peg loops while the other two were fitted with 20-foot nylon cords.

When it threatened to rain, we tied off the hood, drove pegs to windward, tied the cords to trees to make a lean-to (or used pack frames for poles and pegged them down if it were treeless); we did what we could about controlling the drainage and wrapped our bags in the ground cloth. Many a short thunderstorm was weathered in this manner, and we once endured two days of solid rain on the shores of Lake Shasta without wetting our bags.

There are endless ways to rig shelter, if you need it badly and didn't bring a tent, in order to comfortably enjoy what you came for: camping in wild country with your home on your back.

FOUR
Cooking

Backpackers, like armies, travel on their stomachs. If the food doesn't satisfy, the scenery will pale. When cooking becomes a nightmare of confusion and frustration, campers often get decidedly cranky. But if the food is good and the preparation easy the trip tends to go smoothly, even if the ground is hard and the bugs are out in force.

Knowing how to set up the kitchen for efficient operation and make the best use of the food you brought along can make the difference between misery and a successful trip.

Hopefully, you brought along a stove, now considered essential equipment by most backpackers because it provides even, dependable, controllable heat, without the need to build a fireplace, hunt for wood, nurse a fire, fight smoke and falling ashes, and deal with wildly varying heat output that often means scorched or uncooked food, and leaves you with soot-blackened pots. If you brought a stove, hopefully you brought along or memorized the operating instructions. Probably the first consideration before using a stove is to make sure there's ample fuel to complete your meal. Refueling while dinner is underway is dangerous for both you and your dinner, what with the risks of spilling, puncture, explosion and contaminated or badly cooked food.

The second consideration is setting up the stove for maximum stability and shelter. Stability may not seem important until you've had a stove fall over and the dinner you've been hungrily awaiting ends up in the dirt. Most stoves are dangerously wobbly, so take the time to set yours up carefully. Then treat it gingerly during cooking, especially when you first place that heavy pot on the burner.

Sheltering Your Stove

No stove works well—if at all—if not completely sheltered from wind. Few stoves offer even minimally adequate built-in wind protection. It's up to the cook to find a sheltered spot for the kitchen. If none can be found, it must be somehow constructed. The chief ingredients are usually, fallen trees, rocks

dismantling a poorly-located fireplace

or chunks of wood, but don't overlook equipment. A pack on its side, a couple of sleeping bags still in stuff sacks, a foam pad or a folded tarp or ground cloth may be just what you need. Take the time to rig your shelter thoughtfully *before* you start cooking, rather than wait until the meal is half cooked, when you run the risk of knocking over the stove.

All liquid fuel stoves need to be cleaned, some more than others. Cleaning is either manual (with a fine wire that you run through the burner orifice) or built-in (the cleaning needle is integral, operated by a lever or valve). When impurities in liquid fuel cause inevitable clogging, the stove stops or runs poorly until the orifice is reamed out. The recent change in small Optimus gas stoves (Svea 123, 8R and 99) from manual to built-in cleaning has produced some problems. When the valve-activated cleaning needle sticks or runs off the track the flame is diminished or the stove is reluctant to shut off. The solution is to remove the burner with the wrench provided, turn the stove over so the needle assembly falls out, replace the burner and rely in the future on manual cleaning.

Since all stoves are designed for maximum heat output, there are a number of operating hazards that the user should be aware of. In gas stoves the principal dangers occur during refueling. Funnels overflow, fuel bottles get knocked over, gas gets spilled on a hot stove, fuel tanks get too hot, campfires

half dug-out fireplace

prevailing wind →

dug out area

ignite nearby gasoline supplies, the cook panics during a flareup and knocks over the stove, burning himself and catching the tent on fire, a fuel check while cooking causes burnt fingers, a spill or a flare-up. Never forget that gas stoves can explode and spilled fuel can ignite in a flash. Because kerosene is far less volatile, all or most of these hazards are much reduced or nonexistent in kerosene stoves. But since the stove is red hot you can still get burned if you are less than cautious, and spilled kerosene can still burn up your tent.

Stove Hazards

Butane and propane stoves, because they're simple, are considered safe by many campers—and this is a dangerous assumption. Cartridge type stoves are just as dangerous as gas stoves, but the dangers are different, often unpredictable and less dramatically evident. Punctured canisters can turn into torches if ignited or foul your pack if undetected on the trail. And removing a canister that's defective or not yet empty, I can say from personal experience, can freeze your skin painfully. On rare occasions defective or poorly connected canisters spout fire like a torch without warning. Empty canisters thrown in the fire can explode, and butane stoves can erupt in tent-burning flareups when the canisters have been shaken vigorously or the temperature is too low.

Butane comes in a low-pressure steel canister which is comparatively light, but the low pressure means that the gas will not vaporize when the temperature is below the freezing point of water (32°F) at sea level. And when butane is cold or the canister is near empty the flow is very poor. So butane is inefficient below 40°F and fails entirely when colder—except at altitude. The higher you go the better butane performs.

Propane is stored under great pressure, which means that flow is excellent in cold weather or when the canister is nearly empty, but canisters must be thick-walled to withstand the pressure. Although burning time is an impressive six hours, they are too heavy (two pounds, full) to be carried by most recreational backbackers. The greatest advantage of butane and propane is that lighting the stove is no more difficult than lighting a kitchen stove that has no pilot. Simply hold a lighted match to the burner an instant *before* turning on the gas.

Any kind of stove will produce dangerous levels of carbon monoxide if run in an enclosed space (tent). Carbon monoxide is sneaky stuff, invisible, almost odorless. The product of incomplete fuel combustion, it reduces the blood's ability to transport oxygen. Since high altitude has the same effect, it can be seen that the two are additive: the higher you are the more lethal carbon monoxide poisoning will be.

If tent ventilation isn't vigorous—as when buttoned up tightly against wind or storm—a burning stove consumes nearly all the oxygen, causing the occupants of the tent to sweat, gasp and complain of headache and nausea. The danger is greatest in tube, Goretex or sealed fabric tents without vents. It is likewise greatest with the larger stoves, owing to their greater energy output and greater oxygen consumption. Pans so close to the burner that they deform the flame also contribute to incomplete combustion and therefore carbon monoxide production. If you cook in the tent, what you imagine to be high altitude sickness may, at least in part, be carbon monoxide poisoning. Beware!

Stove Lighting Tips

Kerosene stoves can be lighted without a priming fuel by creating a wick. A twisted square of toilet paper tucked into a circle in the kerosene-filled spirit cup will light easily enough. But solid or paste primers are safer, cleaner and much easier to use. And their value goes up if you must cook in a tent. Dependable primers include ESBIT fuel pellets, Optimus priming paste, Heat Tabs, Fire Ribbon and Hexamine. Avoid

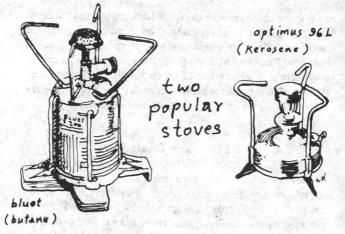

optimus 96 L
(kerosene)

two
popular
stoves

bluet
(butane)

lighter fluid, which is just as dangerous as white gas.

The mention of a few specific stoves and their quirks may help you deal more effectively with yours. The best all round choice at this writing is the Coleman Peak 1, in case you're new to stoves or dissatisfied with what you have. The MSR is marvelous for melting snow by the bucket, but its simmering control is very poor and the stove is fussy at less than full throttle. The Optimus 8R, 99, and Svea 123—in fact, all white gas stoves without pumps—require priming to start, and performance drops in the cold and at high altitude when pressure inside the fuel tank is difficult to maintain. Never fill the tank more than three quarters full and never use the stove when it's near empty or the wick will char and refuse to draw sufficient gas to the burner. Never force the built-in cleaning needle or trouble will follow. Dismantle the mechanism to get it unstuck. Beware the Bleuet S2000S's collapsible base, which can collapse during cooking if not locked in place.

Veteran backpackers have learned that, besides sheltering the stove from all but the faintest zephyr, they can increase cooking efficiency by always using tight fitting lids. It also may be possible to reduce the space between pot and burner to about a quarter inch (optimum) by bending or otherwise modifying the stove's pot supports. If part of your stove's burner will not stay lit or the flame blows out from under your pot, there is a serious loss of efficiency that will waste fuel, prolong cooking time or prevent complete cooking. Move the stove or build a better windbreak, immediately.

Fireplace Design

The alternative to carrying a stove, of course, is to build one out of native material and gather native fuel to fire it. My favorite cooking fireplace design is the half-dugout. There are two advantages: smaller, flatter rocks can be used to insure a more stable structure, and the fire is easier to light and easier to protect from wind. If I were faced with rebuilding a heap of blackened rocks into an efficient cookstove—assuming the location is appropriate and safe—I would first clear a circle about four feet across and sort through the rocks in hopes of finding a matched pair about the size and shape of bricks. Such rocks are never to be found, of course, so I settle for the best I can find (concave upper surfaces are better than convex).

Using the direction of the breeze, the lay of the land and the pattern of branches on nearby trees to determine the path of the prevailing wind, I place my rocks parallel to that path and also to each other—about a foot apart. On the downwind end, I place a larger rock (or rocks) to form a chimney, so the resulting structure forms a squat "U." Then, using a sharp rock fragment as a trowel, I excavate about four inches of earth and charcoal from inside the pit. Now I am ready to place my lightweight grill across the opening, supporting it on the two "bricks" as close as possible to the chimney. Care must be taken to see that it is solid and will not slide or wobble—or my dinner may end up in the fire!

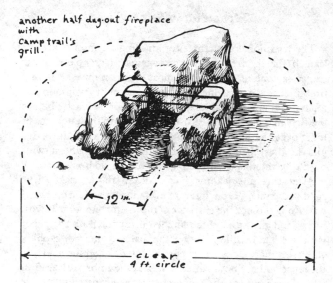

another half dug-out fireplace
with
camp trail's
grill.

12 in.

clear
4 ft. circle

I like to set my grill about two inches above ground level and six inches above the bottom of the firepit, but the proportions must sometimes be altered. On a windy day, I dig deeper and sometimes have to block the windward end with rocks to control the draft. Where there are no rocks at all and the grill sits directly on the ground, the firepit must be deeper still. Inexperienced stove builders invariably build too large a firebox and set the grill much too high. Increasing grill height from six to ten inches probably triples the volume of wood needed to cook dinner. Small fires are easier on the cook, easier on the wood supply and heat is more easily regulated Expert backpackers emulate the Indian and try to cook their food with the smallest fire possible.

Firebuilding Strategies

The traditional structures for kindling a camp fire are the lean-to (match-sized twigs leaned against a larger piece) or the teepee (a cone of twigs). The most common mistake among firebuilders is not having good quantities of dry twigs, tinder, toilet paper and burnables of all sizes within easy reach before the first match is struck. I usually start with three squares of toilet paper loosely crumpled, cover that with a handful of dry pine needles, then build a tepee of the smallest, lightest twigs by tilting them against the paper from all sides.

After carefully leaning half a dozen finger sized sticks against the pile, I crouch low to block the prevailing breeze (if it is strong, I block the entrance to the fire pit temporarily with rocks) and thrust a lighted kitchen match beneath the paper with one hand while I shelter the match from stray zephyrs with the other. Once the paper is lighted, I add the match to the tepee and use both hands to shelter the embryo blaze until all the wood has caught. Care must be taken not to put the fire out by knocking down the tepee with fresh wood, by skipping the intermediate-sized sticks and adding heavy branches, or by letting the tepee burn up before adding fresh wood.

Cooking Tools

Frying pans or griddles are a nuisance for the backpacker because they require a wood fire which blackens them and thus require a heavy cloth or plastic case. Decent frying pans and griddles are not light because heavy gauge metal is needed to evenly spread the heat and prevent burning. The best compromise for the backpacker is a shallow eight or nine inch pan of thin steel or thicker aluminum, with either a ridged or waffled interior to spread heat, or a teflon coating to prevent sticking. Or cook your trout in the ashes—after first wrapping them in foil.

foil ···· pie pan oven ···· hot coals

office clamps ···· ···· pie pans

Though its use requires more experimentation and fiddling, an oven made from two aluminum pie pans fastened together with two spring stationary clamps and suspended over a bed of coals is far lighter and cheaper and nearly as effective. Coals must also be spread on the top pan and covered with a piece of aluminum foil. Most experienced backpackers using easily prepared dishes forget about table knives and forks and carry only a soup spoon apiece and a good-sized simple pocketknife.

A knife is an absolute necessity in the wilds, but knives have become so fashionable that some people carry far more knife than they need. Buck and other expensive heavy knives are status symbols for some, and many rationalize a need to carry (preferably in a leather holster) Swiss army knives (or imitations) that offer a bewildering assortment of heavy, bulky rarely-used gadgets. The knife I like best has a big, broad blade suitable for spreading crackers and cutting salami—and a shorter, slimmer sharply pointed blade for cleaning trout. Brightly colored handles help prevent loss. If I am traveling alone, I put a tiny single-bladed spare jackknife in the outside pack pocket containing the first aid or fishing kit.

Every backpacker needs a cup, and the more experienced choose large ones and dispense with plates. I like a 12-ounce plastic cup which costs 40¢, weighs only 1½ ounces, retains food heat, cleans easily and, when the bottom of the handle is cut, snaps more securely to a belt or nylon line.

All kitchenware must be washed daily to prevent the formation of bacteria that can cause debilitating stomach illness. A few people scrupulously boil everything in soapy water after every meal; many only scrape out pots and pans and rinse in cold water—and cross their fingers. My procedure lies somewhere in between. For a short 2-3 man trip, I carry a 4-inch square abrasive scouring cloth and a 3-inch square sponge backed with emery cloth. Both are soapless. For burned pot bottoms I take a "chore girl" and I always take a dish cloth. Completing my kit are a vial of liquid bio-degradable soap—which is very effective at cleaning skin as well as pots—and a clean diaper or small absorbent hand towel. Old threadbare towels are inefficient. Fire blackened pots are best wiped with wet paper towels, rinsed and allowed to dry before being packed away in plastic or cloth bags. And if you rub a pot with soap before putting it on the fire, the soot will come off with comparative ease.

Eat Constantly

Having set up the kitchen, it's time to look at food, its preparation and eating. To eat well and happily in the wilds, one must set aside the rigid and ritualized habits of urban eating (like the stricture to eat three square meals and not to snack between them) and adopt, instead, an entirely different set of rules. For instance, the principal purpose of wilderness eating is to keep the body fueled and fortified and capable of sustained effort. Energy production, ease of preparation and lightness of weight must all take precedence over flavor. Actually, a thick hot dehydrated stew at the end of a strenuous day often tastes better than a juicy steak in the city.

A backpacker's tastes usually change in the wilds. The body's needs are altered by heavy outdoor exertion, and these needs frequently are reflected in cravings for carbohydrates (liquids, salty foods and sweets), and a corresponding disinterest in other foods (like fats, meat and vegetables). In-

dividual meals lose much of their significance. To keep the body continuously fueled, the backpacker should eat or nibble almost constantly. Many snacks and small meals provide better food digestion, which means better utilization and energy production, than several large meals. A backpacker who makes it a rule not to let an hour pass without eating a little something will enjoy more energy and less weariness and hunger.

As *Freedom of the Hills* puts it, "As soon as breakfast is completed the climber commences lunch, which he continues to eat as long as he is awake, stopping briefly for supper." I generally start nibbling an hour or two after breakfast if I am hiking, and I eat two lunches instead of one, the first in late morning and another in mid-afternoon. I know hikers who go a step further to escape food preparation altogether: they abolish distinct meals, eating every hour and fixing a larger or hot snack when they feel the need.

Drink Often

A hiker living outdoors should drink at least as often as he eats. If he is shirtless or the weather is warm his body may easily lose a gallon of water in a day! Since dehydrated food absorbs water from the body after it is eaten, still more water is needed. A backpacker can scarcely drink too much—provided he takes only a little at a time. Severe dehydration results if most of the fluids lost during the day are not replaced before bedtime.

Since water loss means salt loss, salty foods are unusually welcome. Although the body replaces salt lost normaly, continuous, excessive sweating may justify taking salt tablets. A salt deficiency (from extreme water loss) can result in nausea, aches or cramps. But overdosing on salt is dangerous too. To protect yourself, take no more than two salt tablets with every quart of water you drink. To purify suspect water, boil it or add a trace of iodine. Halazone will not kill the bugs found in really bad water such as that found in the jungle, in primitive countries and downstream of any habitation.

Since heating food greatly increases preparation, requires weighty equipment (pots, stove) and provides only psychological benefit—cooking only reduces nutritive value—more than a few backpackers avoid cooking in the wilds altogether. They find the saving in time, labor and weight more than offsets the lack of comforting warmth.

Keep Menus Simple

Unless you're a gourmet and came to cook, you'll be well advised to keep your food list and its preparation as simple as possible. In my view the importance of easy preparation can scarcely be over-emphasized. After a long hard day on the trail in bad weather, the weary, starving backpacker, crouched in the dirt over an open fire in the cold, wind and dark needs all the help he can get. At such times boiling a pot of water and dumping in the food can be heavy, demanding, exasperating work.

One of the best ways to enjoy simpler, better eating next trip is to take notes this trip. By writing down my thoughts (see the back of this book) on surpluses, insufficiencies, failures, and unfulfilled cravings, I produce a record that makes planning food for the next trip twice as easy. Why start

making dinner — the hard way

from scratch every time? By making notes—and keeping them—food lists are continually refined, the planning ordeal is greatly reduced and you eat better each trip.

Since backpacking is decidedly strenuous, it is hardly surprising that the body's fuel intake must increase significantly in order to keep up with demand. The body's energy requirements and the energy production of food are both measured in calories. It takes twice as many calories to walk at 3 mph as it does to walk at 2 mph. Walking at 4 mph doubles the calorie requirements again, and it takes 2½ times as many calories to gain a 1000 feet of elevation as it does to walk at 2 mph. A variety of studies have shown that —depending on innumerable factors (like body and pack weight, distance covered, terrain, etc.)— it takes 3000-4500 calories a day to keep a backpacker fueled. Easy family trips might require 2000-2500 while climbers may need 5000.

Backpackers who take in fewer calories than their systems need will find the body compensates by burning fat to produce energy. Stored fat is efficiently converted to fuel at the rate of 4100 calories per pound. The backpacker who burns 4000 calories, but takes in only 3590 (410 fewer), will theoretically make up the difference by burning a tenth of a pound of body fat, although individuals vary widely where fat conversion is concerned.

Backpackers unused to strenuous exercise will usually lose weight, but probably not from lack of caloric energy. Exposure to the elements results in water loss, and the change from the high bulk diet of civilization to low bulk dehydrated foods tends to shrink the stomach. For most people, a little hunger and a loss of weight is beneficial to health and need not be construed as the first signs of malnutrition—as long as energy levels remain ample.

Change Your Eating Habits

In the city we customarily eat till we are full. In the wilds, where energy expenditure is far greater, we tend to be anxious about keeping the body fueled; consequently there is a powerful instinct to stuff ourselves with food until we feel comfortably full. In the process it is easy to eat two days' ration at one sitting and get up feeling slightly sick and bloated. The extra power is wasted since the body will not process any more than it can use. It requires some knowledge of the caloric output of foods and the body's likely needs, but if the traveler can muster the necessary self discipline and restraint, he will discover he can eat less with no loss of energy.

This tendency to overeat, in my experience, is as little recognized as it is fundamentally important. Think back to those trips on which you ran out of food. Instead of trusting the menu you originally devised, you probably decided—on the basis of bulk alone—that you weren't getting enough to eat, so you increased the rations. You damned the company that labeled your dinner "serves four," because it barely filled up two of you. It probably didn't occur to you that there might have been enough calories for four and that you didn't have to eat till you were stuffed. The veteran traveler realizes that the slightly empty feeling in his stomach—and even loss of weight—reflects a healthy lack of bulk, not a dangerous shortage of nourishment.

Weight is usually about the same for both dehydrated and freeze-dried foods, since both processes leave about 5% water and 25% of original weight, but dehydrated foods take 2-3 times as long to rehydrate (soak), a severe drawback when you're ravenous even before you stop to camp for the night. Air dried food contains as much as 25% water. I'm willing to simmer my pre-cooked, fresh-tasting freeze-dried stew for 20 minutes at high altitude, but an hour (and sometimes two!) is too long to wait for a less appetizing air-dried dinner to cook.

When it comes to shelf life, it's the packaging that counts. Food in polyethelene bags is always good for a year, but the safe maximum is two years. Vacuum packed foods in foil are good indefinitely—as long as the seal isn't broken. When the vacuum goes (easily determined visually) shelf life drops to the polyethelene level. Food vacuum packed in nitrogen in cans has no known shelf life limit, except for high fat foods (butter, buttermilk, peanut butter powders) which have a five year life expectancy.

Food is divided into three major components: fats, proteins and carbohydrates, all of which are essential to the back-packer's diet. The ideal proportions are essentially unknown and vary according to the temperature, individual, environ-

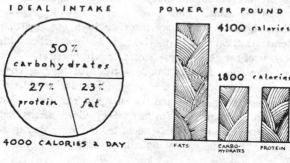

IDEAL INTAKE

50% carbohydrates

27% protein   23% fat

4000 CALORIES a DAY

POWER PER POUND

4100 calories

1800 calories

FATS   CARBO-HYDRATES   PROTEIN

ment and type of activity—but a rule of thumb suggests that caloric intake be roughly 50% carbohydrates, 25-30% protein and 20-25% fats.

Eat Less Meat

The National Academy of Sciences says we eat 50% more protein than we can utilize. Protein serves only to maintain existing muscle. On a rigorous trip, all that's needed is .015 ounces per pound of body weight per day. That means a 100 pound woman needs only an ounce and a half, while her 200 pound boyfriend needs a mere three ounces. More than that is wasted!

Fats are no easier to digest than proteins, but they supply more than twice the energy and release it gradually over a long period of time. The principal fat sources for backpackers are oil, butter, margarine, nuts, meat fat and cheese. The digestion of protein and fat demands the full attention of the body's resources for a considerable period of time. Consumption should be spread through breakfast, lunch and snacks rather than being concentrated in a heavy dinner. Even relatively small amounts should not be eaten before or during strenuous exercise. The blood cannot be expected to circulate rapidly through exercising muscles and digest complex food in the stomach at the same time without failing at one function or the other—usually both.

When heavy demands are made on both the digestion system and the muscles, the body is likely to rebel with shortness of breath, cramps, nausea and dizziness. The first signs are low energy and fatigue. Carbohydrates may conveniently be thought of as pure energy. Digestion is rapid, undemanding and efficient and the energy is released within minutes of consumption. But fast energy release means that carbohydrates are completely exhausted of their power in as little as an hour, and more must be ingested if the energy level

lunchtime..

is to be maintained. The backpacker who lives on carbohy-drates must eat almost continuously to avoid running out of fuel. The common sources of carbohydrate are fruits, cereals, vegetables, starches, honey and sugars.

Since fat digestion yields the most heat, it makes sense in cold country to partake just before retiring on a cold night for leisurely digestion while you sleep. There is no more potent source of fat calories than cooking oil, so I take a pull on the bottle or pour a dash in the stew when calories are needed and there's time for digestion.

Try Spice Power

Some of the strategies I employ may help you to better eating in the wilds. I use the creative addition of spices and condiments to simple dishes to produce variety without com-plicating food preparation. For instance, on a relatively short easy trip, I might increase both the power and the flavor of a packaged stew by adding several of the following: freeze-dried sliced mushrooms, a pinch of Fines Herbs (spice mix), a gob of butter or margarine, parsley flakes, onion or garlic powder, a lump of cheese, crumpled bacon bar or vegetable bacon bits, tabasco sauce, and so forth. I could eat the same basic stew for a week but enjoy a different flavor every night by the restrained use of these and other seasonings. Or take another of my staple foods, applesauce. I keep it exciting day after day by the judicious use of: cinnamon, raisins, lemon powder, vanilla, chopped dates, nutmeg, ginger, nuts, honey and coconut in varying combinations.

On a long hard trip, seasonings and spices become even more vital in the battle against boring, bland meals. A dash or two of chili powder and a shake of onion flakes will turn a dreary pot of beans into spicy chili. A little curry powder will liven up the rice. Jazz up a dreary casserole with dry mustard and Worcestershire sauce. If trout are on the menu, I briefly shake the dampened fish in a plastic bag containing a few ounces of my cornstarch, cornmeal, salt, pepper, onion and garlic powder mix before frying. Trout are also good baked in a butter sauce with sage and basil.

Other versatile ingredients include: sunflower and sesame seeds, slivered almonds, fruit crystals, wheat germ, coriander, bouillon cubes, tomato, beef and chicken base, peanuts, banana flakes, various freeze-dried fruits and vegetables, bay leaves, and oregano. For many years, I carried an old tin spice can filled with a mixture of three parts salt and one each of pepper, onion, garlic and celery salts. It is still one of my favorite shakers.

Kitchen Techniques

I sometimes get rid of leftovers and simultaneously fortify my dinner soup with a gob of butter or a slosh of cooking oil and perhaps some bacon bar or TVP. Any leftover jerky or milk powder may also get dumped in the soup. We cook it in our one big pot and drink it out of our oversized plastic cups, accompanied with a few crackers from the lunch supply. When there is still half an inch of soup in the pot (for flavor)

I empty in a freeze dried dinner and stir in the required amount of cold water. This is contrary to the directions on the package which call for adding boiling water, but by mixing ingredients before heating I maximize valuable soaking time. At 8,000 feet the time needed to rehydrate the casserole may be twice the five minutes advertised, and twenty minutes is better than ten if you don't like your meat hard and rubbery. When the meal is half cooked (i.e. the meat portion is no longer rock hard) I add my salt and pepper mix (to taste), mushroom slices, fine herbs mix (with restraint) and whatever other flavors or fortifications that seem appropriate on that particular evening.

With the aid of big spoons we eat the resulting stew in our unwashed soup cups. The moment the pot is empty and scraped, I fill it with water to simplify future cleaning because experience has taught me that stew allowed to dry will set up like concrete! Once the stew is off the stove a small pot or tea-kettle containing about three cups of water goes on—saving stove fuel. When the water is half heated we use a little in our empty cups to clean out the grease, polishing with a piece of paper towel. Into the hot water goes applesauce, probably premixed with cinnamon and nutmeg. By the time a few raisins and a dash of honey have been stirred in, this pre-cooked dish is ready for consumption in the clean soup-stew cups. The final course is hot tea, along with snack foods, and it

continues until bedtime. I try to remind myself that what I'm eating is low on bulk but dehydrated and concentrated: so I must drink lots of liquids and restrain myself from the urge to eat until full.

Instant Cheer

Except for beer in warm weather I'm not a drinking man, but I've learned that a small belt of something potent can be marvelously beneficial under certain circumstances. Spirits are low at the end of a hard day when you ease the pack off weary shoulders and grimly contemplate setting up camp and cooking dinner in the wind and dark. At such a time, nothing restores cheer by blotting out discomfort like a shot of pain-killer, even if you don't drink.

Only oils and animal fats surpass butter and margine (about 720 calories per 3½ ounces) as a source of fat. Served in Sherpa tea at breakfast, on bread or crackers at lunch, and in soup or stew at dinner, butter palatably provides an ideal source of high yield, long-lasting energy. Parkay offers margarine in a lock-top plastic squeeze bottle designed for camping.

With all the good inexpensive dehydrated food available in the markets nowadays, there's no excuse for carrying canned foods into the wilderness. In some areas glass and cans are now banned.

On the face of it, Instant Breakfast and its relatives like Tiger's Milk should be ideal for backpacking, but my friends and I have reluctantly abandoned them because they dependably produce diarrhea within an hour if we are hiking.

A few drops of vanilla or a little coffee or cocoa mix help mask the slightly artificial flavor of reconstituted milk products.

I generally carry a small plastic bottle of cooking oil, even though I am not equipped to fry, and use it to fortify stews and other dishes when there is leisure for fat digestion. And I sometimes take a pull on the bottle before retiring on especially cold nights.

Molasses, though nearly 25% water, quickly converts to energy and is used like honey or jam by those who like the strong sweet flavor. And a teaspoon or two works beautifully as a gentle natural food laxative—often necessary after a change from city fare to a steady diet of low bulk, dehydrated food.

Although sticky, heavy and liquid, honey behaves well enough in a sturdy screw-capped squeeze bottle or tube. There is no quicker source of potent carbohydrate energy (300 calories per 3½ oz.), and honey is only 17.2% water. It's sweet delicate flavor makes it valuable as a spread, dessert, syrup, frosting and sweetener for drinks.

If you'd like to know more about menu planning, recipes, specific foods, stove selection and cooking equipment, see the Food & Cooking chapters of my *Pleasure Packing for the 80's*.

Eat often, well and with a minimum of fuss, and you're bound to enjoy a satisfying trip.

FIVE
Navigating

*The Compass Game... Itinerary Options...
Get Off the Trail... How Fast Will I Go?...
Start Off Easy... Getting Lost... Ways to
Find North... Getting Found... My Survival Kit*

Since you're already out in the country, it's too late to advise
you to read a book on wilderness navigation before you set
forth. I just hope you're at least somewhat acquainted with the
country you're visiting and have brought along the
appropriate map(s), hopefully a compass of some sort and
maybe a guidebook to the area—especially if you plan to go
cross country. But even if you never plan to leave the well-
worn, well-signed trail, you need to be able to figure out where
you are at all times, and that means reading maps. Ideally,
you've brought along a large scale topographical map to
provide a maximum of detail and a smaller scale map that
shows a large area for identifying distant landmarks.

The first principle of map use is orientation—lining up the
map with the country. The traveler simply spreads out his
map with the compass on top so that north points directly to
the top of the sheet. The map and compass are then turned as a
unit until the north needle points directly to north. When the

magnetic declination (difference between true and magnetic north) is set off (it is shown on all topo maps) the map will be oriented.

When one's position is known and the map is oriented, it becomes easy to identify visible features of the countryside by transferring line-of-sight bearings to the map by means of a straight edge. When only one's general location is known, but several landmarks have been positively identified, it is possible to discover one's precise location by transferring line-of-sight bearing to two known landmarks onto the map. The intersection lines reveal the compassman's exact location. This won't work, of course, where convenient landmarks can't be seen.

The Compass Game

The competent woodsman or mountaineer always tries to develop some inner orientation to make him independent of his compass. To this end, my friends and I play a game on the trail— while taking a rest—that has proven both amusing and instructive. Each of us draws a line in the dirt toward what he believes is true north. Then the compass is brought out, the declination marked off, and the winner declared. The next time the game is played the previous session's winner must draw first. It is surprising how quickly this game develops a sharp sense of direction.

Reading the rise and fall of the land on a topo map is more a matter of practice than talent. The best place to begin is with solitary peaks or hills where the contour lines form concentric circles that get smaller as they go higher toward the summit circle in the center. Widely spaced lines indicate a gentle slope while lines bunched together describe a cliff. Contour lines form arrows that point upstream as they cross water courses and downhill as they descend a ridge or bluff. As one becomes adept at reading topo maps, the actual shapes of landforms

an oriented map:

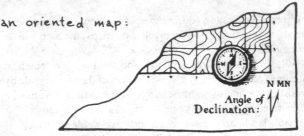

Angle of
Declination:

N MN

begin to materialize on the map so that maps become pictures of the country.

When this happens, topo maps take on a singular fascination. They also become incredibly useful. For instance, by measuring the ups and downs of a trail one can estimate with fair accuracy the time that will be required to traverse a given section of country. This, in turn, allows the trip planner to work out logical camping spots and estimate the time needed for any itinerary. Superior map reading ability is a prime prerequisite for safely visiting the wildest of trailless country. Proficiency with map and compass has saved a great many lives.

Itinerary Options

Presumably, you've made some kid of trip plan or itinerary so that you'll see what you came to see and will get back to the car or civilization before you run out of food and vacation. If your trip plan isn't rigid, consider the main options. Newcomers to the outdoors may want to car camp at the trailhead for a day or two and make exploratory day trips into the wilds until they become acclimated and find an appealing campsite that seems within their reach. Families and other groups with limited range often set up a base camp within an easy walk of the car and then make daily side trips into surrounding country.

Groups with greater mobility or the urge to move may decide to shift their base camp one or more times; others make a practice of packing up and moving every other day. Inexperienced or cautious backpackers often take the shortest route to their goal, then retrace their steps going home. More practiced and imaginative hikers go to some pains to plot a route that makes some kind of circle or loop in order to see more country and avoid treading the same ground twice.

Another popular plan is the shuttle trip. Two cars drive the party to the exit trailhead, where one car is left. Sandwiched into the second car, the party then drives to the entrance trailhead to begin a backpacking traverse between the two. There is also the exotic "double shuttle" in which two traversing parties start at opposite ends of the same route and trade car keys when they pass on the trail, perhaps sharing a meal or camping a night together.

Get Off the Trail

Some backpackers find a greater sense of adventure in deliberately planning no itinerary, going where and when the spirit moves them. Others, similarly motivated, spurn trails altogether in favor of cross-country travel, finding pleasure in avoiding people and the beaten path. Since true wilderness does not begin until the trail has been left behind, it should probably be the goal of most backpackers to travel cross-country, even if only for an hour's day hike from base camp. Wilderness travel means getting off the trail.

I like to start thinking about future trips while I am still in the mountains. I find myself wondering, for instance, whether the rocky, trailless canyon I am passing could be ascended, under pack, to the lake that lies above. As I move along, I try to estimate the difficulty of reaching passes, following ridges and crossing slopes, with an eye toward future trips. I study the topo map to learn what lies on the other side of the mountain and to compare the bunching of contour lines with those on slopes I can see or have already climbed. And I often take pictures of country that interests me for reference in planning future trips.

This type of on-the-spot research becomes invaluable for plotting feasible cross-country routes in trailless country. A glance up a canyon on this year's trip may warn me against including it in the next year's itinerary because the gentle slope suggested by the topo map turns out to be a series of ledges and cliffs. Or I confidently plan a route down a forbidding steep slope because I know it to be an easy sand and scree slide.

How Fast Will I Go?

The question inevitably asked by strangers to the wilderness is how fast will I travel? Or, how far should I plan to go in a day? There are no answers, only generalities. On relatively level trails at moderate elevations, a lightly burdened, long legged well-conditioned man may manage 4 m.p.h. At elevations over 6000 feet in rolling country, a well-acclimated backpacker is moving extremely well if he can cover 3 m.p.h. The average backpacker, fresh from the city, with a full pack, heading up into the mountains will be lucky to average 2 m.p.h. These speeds are for hikers who keep moving and should probably be cut in half for those who want to poke along, smell the flowers, take pictures and enjoy the view.

People who are overburdened or climbing steeply or moving cross country may average only 1 m.p.h. Children, the elderly and hikers strongly affected by the altitude may manage as little as half a mile an hour. A friend of mine has devised a useful formula for predicting his speed. He plans every hour to cover two miles if the trail is flat or mildly descending. For each thousand feet of rise he adds another hour. For steeply descending trail he adds a half hour per

she finds out where she is by triangulating from two known landmarks.

thousand feet, increasing that to a full hour for extremely steep downhill. By plotting a rough profile of the trail from the topo map and applying his formula, he can estimate quite accurately the time needed to walk it with a moderate—under 30 pound—load.

Start Off Easy

How far one should attempt to go in a given day is equally hard to answer. The first day out is always the hardest, especially if the hiker has gained a mile or two of altitude between home and the trailhead, carries a healthy pack and is in less than top physical condition. In these circumstances, five miles may be a full day's work. Well-conditioned backpackers who know their capabilities may cover ten or more miles the first day and not suffer unduly, but most people will be happier if they schedule considerably less. On succeeding days it becomes possible to cover more ground with less discomfort. I have covered 15 or 20 miles on the third or fourth day with greater comfort than I felt after eight miles the first day.

There is no particular virtue in covering great distances. I have received more pleasure, solitude and a sense of wilderness from backpacking less than two miles cross-country into a neglected corner than I have from following sixty miles of well-traveled trail and camping in battered, over-used campsites.

Survival should not be a problem for the backpacker—unless he is hurt or lost. A first aid kit and the ability to use it should enable him to cope with all but the worst accidents and health failures. His equipment, experience and trip preparation should enable him to survive whatever bad weather or minor mishaps befall him with no more than extreme discomfort. It simply isn't possible to protect against all the hazards of wilderness travel. Most people carry too much, not too little. Instead of carrying gadgets or somebody else's list of essentials, develop self-reliance, build your experience and don't make the same mistake twice.

Getting Lost

Getting lost—or thoroughly confused—is not uncommon in the wilds and rarely leads to tragedy if sensible procedures are followed. I have been unsure of my location a good many times without suffering unduly. The lost backpacker's ability to regain his sense of direction and rediscover his location (or make himself easy to find) depends largely on his ability to control panic and fear so that logic and reason can prevail.

The best insurance I know against getting lost in strange country is to study it as I move along. I consult the map and reorient myself with each new turning of the trail. I identify and study the configuration of new landmarks as they appear. I frequently look backward over the country just traversed to see how it looks going the other way. If I am traveling cross-country or on an unmapped trail, I stop several times each mile to draw the route on my map. And at critical points (stream crossings, trail branchings, confusing turns), I make appropriate entries in my notebook.

A compass is the easiest means of orientation, but the sun, the stars and the time can also be used to determine direction—and to act as a check on the compass. More than a few disasters result when lost travelers refuse to accept what their compasses tell them. Unaware that they are lost and convinced they have their bearings, they assume the compass is broken or being unnaturally influenced.

Incidentally, precision compasses rarely are needed in wild country simply because it's impossible for the hiker to measure distance accurately and maintain precise bearings. One degree of error in a mile amounts to only 92 feet, so compasses that can be read to the nearest five degrees will be accurate enough for most purposes. In strange country where landmarks are unfamiliar, a compass is no less than indispensable. Many times I have worked out my true location or avoided a wrong turn by referring to a dollar-sized compass that weighs a fraction of an ounce and cost less than a dollar.

Ways To Find North

A roughly accurate watch will function as a compass on any day that the sun is out. If one turns the watch so that the hour hand points toward the sun, true south will lie halfway between the hour hand and the number twelve. An allowance must be made if the watch is set on Daylight Saving time, which is generally an hour earlier than standard (or sun) time.

If the time is known generally, even if only within two hours, a rough but very useful idea of direction can be obtained simply by knowing that (in western America) the summer sun rises a little north of due east, stands due south at noon (standard time), and sets a little north of due west. In the winter the sun's path lies considerably to the south, rising south of east and setting south of west. Early and late in the

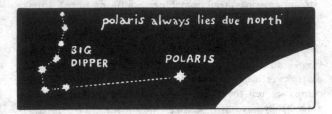

day, one can easily determine directions with sufficient accuracy for most purposes.

Another useful strategy involves pushing a stick vertically in the ground, marking the end of its shadow, waiting about 15 minutes then marking the shadow again. A line between the two marks will run east-west (the first mark is the west end). A line drawn at right angles will run north-south.

If the night is reasonably clear (in the northern hemisphere), it is relatively easy to find the North Star (Polaris) which is never more than one degree from true north. Its location is determined from the Big Dipper (or Big Bear), a bright and easily identifiable constellation nearly always visible in the northern sky. A line drawn upward from the outermost stars at the bottom and lip of the cup will point to Polaris (see drawing). In the southern hemisphere, the long axis of the Southern Cross points toward a starless region that lies due south. The prominent constellation Orion lies in a nearly north-south plane, and the uppermost of the three stars in the belt rises due east and sets due west—from any point on the face of the earth.

Getting Found

There are so many variables in every situation that it is difficult to advise the backpacker who has managed to get lost. However a few general rules nearly always apply. The novice hiker has a tendency to plunge on through country that has gradually grown unfamiliar in hopes of reaching a familiar landmark. The veteran backpacker will resist this impulse, stop, admit to himself that he is at least temporarily lost, and sit down to review the situation. When he has overcome the anxiety that often accompanies such an admission, he will rationally review the situation, carefully considering all the information available.

After studying the map and thinking carefully, he may find a landmark he can identify that will reveal his approximate position. Or thinking back over the country he has traversed he may feel that by retracing his steps he can return to a known point in a comparatively short time. After all the evidence has been sifted, the important decision is whether to try and return to a known point, whether to stay put and await rescue, or whether to head hopefully toward civilization. Only full consideration of the situation in a rational, panic-free manner will reveal the best course of action. The backpacker well equipped for recreational travel is generally well equipped for survival. Dayhikers are not so well provisioned and ought to carry, in addition to a good first aid kit, something that might be called a survival kit.

My Survival Kit

The one I carry in my creel or daypack whenever I go out (in addition to the small first aid kit) consists of an ancient tin cup, which can be used for cooking, a dozen kitchen matches,

day-pack
survival
kit

first aid essentials ...

a yard and a half of toilet paper, about fifty feet of 550 lb. test nylon cord, a tiny one-bladed knife, two heavy-duty plastic bags, a quarter of a rum fudge bar broken into squares, three tea bags, three bouillon cubes, note paper and the stub of a pencil. All these items pack in the cup which in turn is packed in one of the plastic bags. Total weight is only six ounces.

There are many more items that might be worth carrying. A small waterproof match box with built-in compass and whistle might be worthwhile. So might the three ounce, 56" x 84" Rescue Blanket which is strong and a good reflector. In harsher seasons, when accidents can prove more dangerous, considerably more survival (and backpacking) gear can be justified. Fire starters, for instance, are part of my basic equipment when traveling in country that is cold, wet or otherwise unfriendly.

In mild summer weather, if adversity fails to strike, I can always use my survival kit to brew a cup of tea beneath the shelter of a tree while I wait for an afternoon thunderstorm to pass.

If you'd like to know more about compass selection and use, trip planning, and conditioning programs, see the Getting Ready chapter in my *Pleasure Packing for the 80's*.

Once again let me urge you to make brief notes (in the blank pages that follow) while still in the wilds to record strong feelings that will make future trips more successful. In camp on the last leg of most trips I sit down with my notebook while memories are fresh, and make pertinent notes about the trip. I criticize the food, recording both the noteworthy successes and the dishes that need never be carried again. I might write down, for instance, that breakfasts were a little skimpy so the cereal allotment should be increased from three ounces per meal to four.

By making notes before the memory fades, I accomplish three things: (1) I give myself the best possible chance to increase my enjoyment of future trips, (2) I avoid repeating mistakes for failure to remember them, and (3) by putting it all in writing, I avoid the mental drudgery of having to start planning each trip from scratch. Fifteen minutes spent making notes at the end of a trip will save two hours of preparation a month later.

the
trip-
planner's
friends:

My Basic Checklist

My personal checklist is provided in the hope that out in the wilds it may suggest items you wish you'd brought and vow to bring the next time. Between trips in the city it may help you plan the next one and prevent you from setting forth into the wilderness without something vital.

The checklist takes the place of a perfect memory, and the longer it runs the more security it provides. Every time I buy a new piece of gear, I add it to my checklist, but I rarely can bring myself to cross anything off, even the items I have not dreamed of carrying in years. Like other backpackers, interested in comfort, I enjoy reading other people's lists. The abridged checklist that follows may serve as a starter for newcomers to backpacking—but only as a starter. A checklist is a highly personal thing and the beginner must eventually construct his own, updating it after every trip to make sure it contains every scrap of gear he owns.

PACKS	Pounds-Ounces
Frame and packbag	3-12
Back Magic	5-2
Orange daypack	9
Fanny pack	5½
Belt pack(s)	2

CLOTHING - FOOTWEAR	
Green wind anorak	7½
Straw hat	3
Tennis hat	2
VB shirt	4
VB gloves	
VB socks (Baggies)	
VB Zip Rain Pants	10
String shirt	7
Hickory shirt	10
Moleskin shirt	14

VB-rain storm suit	1-5
Zip-arm pile sweater	1-5
Denim shirt	8
Down sweater	1-1
Hiking shorts	10
Running shorts	2
Bathing suit	5
Stretch rag socks	4
Liner socks	1
Wick Dry socks	3½
Double-zip trousers	1-1
Bandana	¾
Watch cap	2
Balaclava	3
Ben Davis pullover shirt	6
Boxer shorts	3
Odlo long johns	3
Wool mittens	3

Leather gloves	3
Short gaiters	4
DMC GT boots	2-4
Vasque boots	3-4
Go-aheads (sandals)	2
Zip-arm rain parka	1-0

SHELTER

Space rescue blanket	2
Stephenson tent	2-15
GT bivy sack	1-2
Ground cloth (nylon)	12
2-Man tube tent	2-4
Ground cloth (plastic)	12

BEDS

Stephenson bag (thin)	4-2
Zip-lock (foam) bag	5-0
NF superlight bag	3-1
72-In. foam pad	2-0
72-In. Therma-a-Rest	2-8
72-In. Airlift	1-3
72-In. ½" EVA foam	12

KITCHEN GEAR

Pocketknife (big)	2½
2-Blade Swiss army	1
Bleuet with cartridge	1-13
Extra cartridge	10
Peak 1 stove	2-0
Sigg pint bottle	4
Sigg quart bottle	5
Sigg pot, lid	9
Pot tongs	1½
Chore Girl	½
Salt mix shaker	2
Wooden matches	1
Emery cloth-backed sponge	½

Paper towels and TP	2
Plastic cup	1½
Aluminum measuring cup	¾
1-Quart bottle	5
1-Quart Oasis canteen	5
Tea kettle	3
Gallon jug (plastic)	4
Tubular grill	4
Gerry plastic tube	¾
Fork-spoon	1½
Bio-suds	2

MISCELLANEOUS

Dark glasses	1½
Glacier glasses w/band	2
Lip salve	½
Thermometer	½
Compass	2
Altimeter	3½
Maps	1?
50' 550 lb. test cord	3
Cutters snakebite kit	1
Jungle (bug) Juice	2
Notebook, pencil	2
Creel (loaded)	9
Mallory flashlight	3
Lithium headlamp	1-8
First aid kit (large)	9
First aid kit (small)	6
Personal kit	3
Konica (35mm camera)	13
Extra film	2
Fly rod, reel, line	7½
Paperback book	7
Sea & Ski tubelet	1
Plastic garbage bags	1
Candle	1

GOING BACK

When I get back
to the high bright world
of the windblown sun
and the meadowed rock
things will be all right.

When I return
to the mountain wild
on a turning trail
through a summer rain
my rhythm will return.

When I can escape
to a land left wild
on a still starred night
drowned deep in peace
my life will turn around.

When I get back
to the wilds again
and the easy peace
of a dreaming fire
I'll be content again.

NOTES

What to bring more of, what to leave home,
what to do differently...

NOTES

NOTES

NOTES

NOTES

NOTES

NOTES

NOTES